Unions and Legitimacy

Unions and Legitimacy

Gary Chaison

Barbara Bigelow

ILR Press

An imprint of

Cornell University Press

Ithaca and London

First published 2002 by Cornell University Press

Printed in the United States of America

Library of Congress Cataloging-in-Publication Data
Chaison, Gary N.
    Unions and legitimacy / Gary Chaison, Barbara Bigelow.
       p. cm.
Includes bibliographical references and index.
    ISBN 0-8014-3512-9 (cloth : alk. paper)
    1. Labor unions—Recognition—United States.   2. Consensus
(Social sciences)—United States.   I. Bigelow, Barbara Jane, 1951–
II. Title.
    HD6490.R42 U5415 2001
    331.89'12'0973—dc21   2001003446

Cornell University Press strives to use environmentally responsible suppliers and materials to the fullest extent possible in the publishing of its books. Such materials include vegetable-based, low-VOC inks and acid-free papers that are recycled, totally chlorine-free, or partly composed of nonwood fibers. Books that bear the logo of the FSC (Forest Stewardship Council) use paper taken from forests that have been inspected and certified as meeting the highest standards for environmental and social responsibility. For further information, visit our website at *www.cornellpress.cornell.edu.*

Cloth printing   10 9 8 7 6 5 4 3 2 1

To Joanne

and

Robyn, Emily, and Lissa

CONTENTS

ACKNOWLEDGMENTS

Nearly a decade ago we joined a colleague at Clark University, Ed Ottensmeyer, in an attempt to use organization theory to shed light on the predicament of contemporary labor unions. We were responding to an invitation to submit a paper to a special issue of *Research in the Sociology of Organizations* devoted to industrial relations. Our collaboration produced the first application of the concept of legitimacy, as it was being developed in organization theory, to labor unions. We found that the unions' problems with legitimacy helped explain the apparent inertia of the labor movement in a time of crisis. Our basic research framework was discussed in 1991 at the national meetings of the Academy of Management. Two years later our paper was published, and we also presented our concepts and conclusions to an audience of top union staff at the annual meeting of the National Union Administrators Group.

These are the roots of the present book. We were so impressed by the power of legitimacy that we decided to continue our research on a grander scale and in a new direction. Our belief was that we could use legitimacy as a lens for seeing the labor movement anew, for explaining the causes of recent union successes and failures. We sought to refine and advance the conceptual foundation of our earlier work and, through a series of cases, understand how unions manage different forms of legitimacy with different constituencies. Legitimacy, we argue, matters a great deal to unions; it should lie at the very heart of the debates within the labor movement and in academic circles about their future direction.

We are greatly indebted to the many people who helped us. Union staff generously shared their insights and information. Special thanks to Mark Anderson of the AFL-CIO's Food and Allied

Services Trade Department, Candy Brown of the AFL-CIO Union Privilege, Bill Fletcher of the Service Employees International Union, Donovan King of the American Federation of State, County, and Municipal Employees, and George Kohl of the Communications Workers of America. We are tremendously impressed by the labor relations skills and dedication to the nursing profession of the officers and staff of the Massachusetts Nurses Association (MNA). We are grateful to Mary Manning (the MNA's president), David Schildmeier (director of public relations), and Julie Pinkham (director of labor relations) for meeting with us and generously sharing information and impressions.

Margarete Arndt, our friend and colleague at Clark University's School of Management, could always be counted on for sound advice. As we mentioned earlier, another colleague, Ed Ottensmeyer, worked with us on the initial study of union legitimacy and helped create the framework for the present volume. Ellen Dannin (California Western School of Law) and Susan Eaton (Massachusetts Institute of Technology) always responded helpfully to our inquiries about labor law and labor unions. Of course, all the usual caveats apply; we are solely responsible for our interpretations and conclusions.

Diane Adams of Clark's Graduate School of Management fielded our editorial questions with her customary expertise. Frances Wychorski provided valuable assistance in the hard work of revising and processing drafts of the manuscript. Michelle Tei-Mei Jung, Roman Tereshenko, and Natalie Brown were meticulous and enthusiastic research assistants. Clark's Academic Development Fund provided a research grant for our interviews in Washington, D.C.

Two anonymous reviewers selected by Cornell University Press read our proposal and the initial draft of the manuscript; their suggestions improved the depth and breadth of our analysis, and valuable comments from a third reviewer helped us strengthen the manuscript. Our special thanks to Fran Benson of the Press for believing for so long that this book should be written and that we were the ones to write it. Like so many others, we have benefited from Fran's good sense and experience in academic publishing and industrial relations.

Finally, we thank our families for their patience and encouragement. It is not possible to express fully the magnitude of our debt to our families; as a simple but lasting sign of our gratitude, we dedicate this book to them.

Unions and Legitimacy

CHAPTER 1

Legitimacy Matters—But What Is It?

There was no precise moment when the tide began to turn against labor unions in America. There was no single catastrophic event—no landmark strike that was broken, no massive organizing campaign that was turned back, no key negotiation that went poorly for labor. But beyond any doubt, since the early 1980s, unions have lost many of their resources and much of their influence and now find themselves in the midst of a continuing crisis.

Union membership, a popular indicator of the labor movement's condition, has fallen by nearly five million (about one-fourth) since 1980. Much of this loss is in the unions' stronghold of manufacturing, a sector hard hit by foreign competition. Unions, however, have also experienced heavy losses in other areas of traditional strength—construction, transportation, communications—as well as in the lesser-unionized wholesale and retail trade. By the year 2000, only about one in eight workers in private employment was a union member—a proportion similar to that of the early 1930s, before laws were passed protecting workers' rights to join unions. This is among the lowest percentages of all industrialized countries (Chaison and Rose 1991; Burkins 2000).

As membership levels and funds from members' dues have fallen, union leaders have had to cut back on organizing and concentrate on negotiating and enforcing collective agreements. But no matter how difficult to achieve, membership growth is a necessity, not a luxury, for unions. They cannot represent only 14 percent of the workforce, and even less in the future, and effectively represent workers, launch organizing drives, and influence politicians through lobbying. Bronfenbrenner (1998:22) surveyed the dismal organizing landscape and reached a conclusion shared by many: "Either U.S. unions must quickly and effectively organize millions of new workers or face becoming irrevocably marginalized in both the political and economic arenas." While a few unions have been able to pick up the pace of organizing, and have pointed to their successes as the start of a general union revival, most have had persistent difficulty increasing their membership rolls in expanding sectors of the labor force (e.g., service and technical workers) as well as their core occupations and industries (Rose and Chaison 2000).

Those trying to explain union decline frequently mention the unions' loss of legitimacy. For example, the unions' narrow focus on economic rather than political issues is said by some to have been the cause of their declining legitimacy, and thus power, since the 1970s (Murray and Reshef 1988). In a discussion of the insecurity of labor in a world dominated by global product and labor markets, unions are criticized for focusing narrowly on the status and privileges of their members. This limited perspective jeopardizes the unions' legitimacy as the voice of all workers in the much-needed dialogue with employers and state over economic restructuring (Newland 1999). The unions' inability to accommodate internal debate and their leaders' control over dissent since the 1960s have been blamed for the "erosion in the legitimacy of the labor movement as a vital part of American democratic politics" (Lichtenstein 1999:82). And contemporary managers are said to deny the legitimacy of unions by excluding them from important workplace and company decisions (e.g., Barkin 1986; Lawler 1990).

Despite assumptions that legitimacy is important to unions, there is no common understanding of what the legitimacy of unions means or why it matters. The concept of legitimacy, however, has been well developed within organizational theory. In 1993 we linked the concept of organizational legitimacy with research on the unions' crisis and showed how problems of legitimacy help explain unions' inertia in difficult times (Chaison, Bigelow, and Ottensmeyer 1993). Our purpose in this book is to extend that work by using legitimacy to gain a new and powerful perspective on union activities.

To judge solely on its appearance in discussions of unions, legitimacy matters. First, the term is often used to signify conformity with the standards of the federal National Labor Relations Board, that is, the NLRB's certification of unions as bargaining agents after they win the majority support of workers in secret ballot elections. This is the primary way that unions organize workers and compel employers to negotiate with them. Heckscher (1988:47) writes that the union certification process that evolved from the 1935 National Labor Relations Act (Wagner Act) "clearly put the government in the business of *conferring legitimacy* on chosen bodies; it made government, in fact, partly responsible for the *creation* of unions as organizations." Kochan and Katz (1988:76) observed that the legal framework "elevated the system of collective bargaining to new heights of legitimacy in society. From an institution that was once viewed as a criminal conspiracy and then as a monopoly, collective bargaining was transformed into the preferred mechanism for determining wages, hours, and other terms and conditions of employment." It is not surprising, then, that Wolters (1982) found that a majority of the union officers and managers who responded to his survey believed that both the precondition and result of the legitimacy of unions was certification after a favorable vote among employees. Logically, legitimate unions (those enjoying workers' support) became certified, and so certified unions must be legitimate.

Second, legitimacy has been equated with the public approval of unions and what they do, whether in the local community (Craft and Extejt 1983; Cutcher-Gershenfeld 1984) or the general populace (Heckscher 1988; Atanassov 1995). For example, in his comparative study of the core beliefs underlying labor relations systems, Adams (1995) argues that for unions and collective bargaining to be legitimate, they must be shown to be beneficial (or at least not harmful) to the nation as a whole and must allow citizens to participate in decisions affecting their interests. When Moberg (1999) argues that union renewal should be built on increased membership participation, he sees such participation as helping unions gain legitimacy from the general public (as well as their members). Finally, Cornfield (1999:3) reviewing over sixty years of Gallup Polls on the public's approval of unions, concludes that "the public has continuously afforded labor unions substantial legitimacy" and that such legitimacy has withstood changes in union power.

Third, references to the legitimacy of unions are conspicuous in proposals for union-management cooperation and employee participation plans. These arrangements can range from workers' committees for raising production to joint union-management committees that improve workplace safety to the inclusion of union officers on management committees that make strategic decisions. When we hear of the need for increased cooperation and participation, we inevitably learn that this can happen only if management believes in the legitimacy of unions and accepts them as valued advisers in running the workplace (e.g., Collective Bargaining Forum 1999).

In this context, legitimacy means that the employers respect the union as an organization and its role as representative of the workforce (e.g., U.S. Department of Labor 1982; Kochan, Katz, and Mower 1984; Gold 1986; Kochan 1988; Peterson and Tracy 1988). Kochan (1988:28) writes that a precondition to the diffusion of new work processes and innovations in employee participation is that "unions must be accepted by management as legitimate and full partners in the design and guidance of these efforts." Both union and employer participants at a conference on promoting cooperative programs agreed that a major impediment to starting programs is that "management is reluctant to concede the legitimacy of organized labor and to accept it as a partner in production" (U.S. Department of Labor 1982:25). A review of labor-management cooperation in the government sector concludes that "when the legitimacy and the role of the union is not challenged, union leaders can focus their efforts on service improvement. Mutual respect of labor and management leadership is critical to success" (U.S. Secretary of Labor's Task Force 1996:7).

Finally, legitimacy increasingly appears as a variable to be defined, measured, and discussed in industrial relations research. For example, Greenfield and Pleasure (1993) believe that legitimacy and power are the only appropriate yardsticks for determining whether a union is the true voice of the workers it claims to represent. Here legitimacy means that workers freely consent to be represented. Gahan and Bell (1999), two Australian scholars, define legitimacy as the members' support for union strategies and find that such support can be achieved when unions promote both internal democracy and members' loyalty to the union. Legitimacy has also been examined in New Zealand in the context of employers' and the government's campaign to change the basis of employee representation (Harbridge and Honeybone 1996); in Bulgaria as an attribute of emerging and established unions that vie for power in that nation's transitional economy (Atanassov 1995); and in Sweden in terms of the differences in the expected and actual participation of members in their unions (Ahlén 1992, 1995).

Although legitimacy clearly matters, these examples suggest that what it means is not so clear. Legitimacy is defined as conformity to legal standards of union certification, employer respect for and acceptance of unions, and public approval of unions as workplace representatives or as the voice of all working men and women. Writers also refer to different types of legitimacy. For example, Harbridge and Honeybone (1996), studying the changes in the collective bargaining regime in New Zealand, deal with a concept they term "external union legitimacy," which describes the unions' ability to negotiate multi-employer contracts, to have secure and uncontested status at their workplaces, and to be capable of effectively negotiating for members and nonmembers alike. Ahlén (1992, 1995), examining behavioral aspects of a union merger in Sweden, writes of "democratic legitimacy," that is, the extent to which the members' democratic ambitions for their unions' government are met by their personal experience of how decisions are actually made in their unions. A roughly similar measure of legitimacy is used by Gahan and Bell (1999) in their study of membership support and the efficacy of union strategies in an Australian union.

Despite the differences in the uses and definitions of legitimacy, a common thread emerges: legitimacy is conferred by a variety of constituencies and reflects their expectations, whether these involve the unions' conformity to legal standards or the beneficial and valued character of union activities and goals. The definition of legitimacy provided by Suchman (1995:574) in his synthesis of the literature on organizational legitimacy captures these meanings: "Legitimacy is a generalized perception or assumption that the actions of an entity are desirable, proper, or appropriate within some socially constructed system of norms, values, beliefs and definitions."

Suchman (1995:574) offers some helpful clarifications for defining legitimacy. First, legitimacy is generalized because "it represents an umbrella evaluation that, to some extent, transcends specific adverse acts or occurrences." For instance, when Rely brand tampons were blamed for deaths resulting from toxic shock syndrome, Procter & Gamble's legitimacy helped it transcend the crisis (Ashforth and Gibbs 1990). Second, legitimacy is a perception or assumption: it tells us how constituencies see the organization. Third, legitimacy is socially constructed and not dependent on individual values. So long as the collective group (e.g., the local community, consumers, managers) says that the organization is legitimate, the organization can maintain its legitimacy despite concerns of individual observers about some specific behavior.

A primary purpose of this book is to use legitimacy as a lens for examining union activities and to discuss the new insights this analysis provides. Our reasons for studying legitimacy are not only that the term is repeatedly used in discussions of contemporary unions but also that unions operate in a strong institutional environment and display features common to organizations that do so.

Legitimacy matters in institutional environments: organizations that conform to institutionalized practices and procedures have legitimacy and are rewarded with the support of their constituencies. Meyer and his colleagues (Meyer and Rowan 1977; Meyer, Scott, and Deal 1983; Meyer and Scott 1983; Scott and Meyer 1991) have defined institutional environments as organizational environments "characterized by elaborate rules and requirements to which individual organizations must conform if they are to receive support and legitimacy" (Scott and Meyer 1991:123). These rules and requirements stem from a variety of sources—regulatory agencies, accrediting bodies, professional trade associations—as well as from widely shared values and belief systems, all of which "define how specific types of organizations are to conduct themselves" (Scott and Meyer 1991:123). Legitimacy can be as important (and, in highly institutionalized environments, even more important) to an organization's ability to secure resources as its efficiency or market relationships.

Although virtually all organizations operate to some degree in institutional environments, the strength of these environments differs (Scott 1987; Alexander and D'Aunno 1990). For labor unions, the institutional environment is quite strong. There is a well-developed framework of labor laws reflecting the beliefs that the unions' proper role is as a counterweight to employers' power at the workplace. Workers join unions, and labor boards certify unions to negotiate, administer, and enforce legally binding agreements covering wages, hours, and conditions of employment. The collective exercise of power by workers through their union is deemed appropriate because of the lesser power of the individual worker relative to his or her employer. Collective bargaining is likened to a system of self-government by management and labor, a sort of legislature in which both parties, representing their constituencies, debate, compromise, and eventually legislate the rules under which the workplace will be governed (Stone 1981, 1992). Hence, unions function in a legal system that expresses widely shared values about what unions should do and why society should protect or promote union activities.

Union democracy is yet another widely shared value. Democracy is unquestioned as a vital attribute of unions, independent of its impact on union effectiveness. Both the staunchest supporters and harshest critics of unions will agree that unions, as organizations representing members, must act democratically (e.g., by electing officers freely and regularly, allowing members to run for office, having members vote on changes in their union's constitution, and so on). Democracy must prevail even if it reduces union effectiveness by, for example, creating political factions within unions at a time when solidarity is crucial, or delaying action when speed might be important (e.g., by encouraging members to debate increases in union dues or the ratification of collective agreements) (Strauss 1991).

Unions also display features common to organizations that operate in institutional environments. The relationship between means and ends is difficult to measure: there are no objective standards of union success as an organization or worker representative. There is no agreed-on definition of union efficiency in recruiting members, bargaining, and engaging in political activity. Even financial measures of performance are not straightforward; union expenditures measure inputs, not outputs, and show how much money a union can raise rather than how well it uses its funds, that is, how well it performs (Strauss 1975).

In summary, legitimacy matters. Contextually, it is a term frequently used in discussions of union decline. Conceptually, it captures an important element of organizations' access to resources and survival in an institutional environment.

We use three dimensions of legitimacy to analyze union activities: the constituencies that confer legitimacy, the forms of legitimacy, and strategies for managing legitimacy. In chapter 2 we describe the different constituencies. Here we address the forms and strategies.

Legitimacy for any organization is not unidimensional. To illustrate, one reason why banks as institutions are legitimate is that they provide a service that people want. For another, perceptions and expectations about banks are widely shared, and accounts of what a bank should do and how it should be done are fairly clear. When a bank operates consistently with these generalized accounts, it is deemed legitimate. But banks are also taken for granted; that is, they are legitimate not just because they benefit people and their processes, structures, and goals are valued but also because it is virtually unthinkable not to have banks. We assume that there will always be banks in our economy and society, and it is inconceivable that banks would disappear as an institution and their functions be performed by, for example, post offices or convenience stores. Although we might challenge the appropriateness of some of their means and ends, such as discriminatory loans, excessive interest rates, or flashy advertisements, the existence of banks is unassailable.

Suchman (1995) distinguishes among three broad types of legitimacy: pragmatic, moral, and cognitive. Pragmatic legitimacy, the most elementary form, is derived from the self-interested calculations of an organization and its constituencies. The organization is supported because it provides specific favorable exchanges: it gives something valuable and receives something valuable in return. Either the constituencies expect value from their policy of supporting the organization, or they believe that the organization is responsive to their interests. In contrast, moral legitimacy However, "rests not on judgments about whether a given activity benefits the evaluator but rather on judgments about whether the activity is 'the right thing to do'" (Suchman 1995:579). Positive evaluation is based on whether the organization accomplishes something of social value, uses socially acceptable techniques and procedures, or has features or structures that are socially valued. Constituencies confer legitimacy because they perceive the organization to be promoting societal welfare. They consider the organization's structure, process, or outcomes to be "appropriate and right given existing norms and values" (Aldrich and Fiol 1994).

The third form of legitimacy, cognitive legitimacy, evolves from the constituencies' "mere acceptance of the organization as necessary or inevitable" (Suchman 1995:582). Constituents support the organization not because of their own self-interest or social valuation but because of its taken-for-granted character. The organization is beyond dissent. This is "the most subtle and the most powerful source of legitimacy" (Suchman 1995:582). Unlike pragmatic and moral legitimacy, cognitive legitimacy does not involve evaluation. Rather, organizations are simply accepted as necessary or inevitable (Jepperson 1991; Suchman 1995). Churches, schools, fire departments, and hospitals all have cognitive legitimacy. Organizations that manage to attain cognitive legitimacy are unassailable; it is difficult to argue against their presence. This is a rare and rarified status.

Suchman (1995:584–585) draws some crucial distinctions among these forms of legitimacy:

Pragmatic legitimacy rests on audience self-interest whereas moral and cognitive legitimacy do not: audiences base pragmatic assessments largely on self-regarding utility calculations, and organizations can often purchase pragmatic legitimacy by directing tangible rewards to specific constituencies; in contrast, moral and cognitive legitimation implicate larger cultural rules ... As one moves from the pragmatic to the moral to the cognitive, legitimacy becomes more elusive to obtain and more difficult to manipulate, but it also becomes more subtle, more profound, and more self-sustaining, once established.

Pragmatic legitimacy is the easiest to manipulate. Essentially the organization tries to persuade constituents to value what it offers, or it shows how it is responding to their needs. But pragmatic legitimacy alone is a narrow and unsteady foundation; it lacks any ideological underpinning that equates the organization with social values or that establishes it as unassailable. If the organization no longer produces something valuable, or if what constituencies see as valuable changes over time, legitimacy is threatened.

Legitimacy is also a resource that can be managed (Dowling and Pfeffer 1975; Pfeffer and Salancik 1978). Organizations manage legitimacy to achieve one of three purposes: to defend legitimacy when it is threatened or challenged, to gain or extend it when an organization is engaging in a new activity or using new processes or procedures, and to maintain it (Ashforth and Gibbs 1990). While the first two—defending and gaining or extending legitimacy—may appear more overtly difficult, managing legitimacy is always problematic (Ashforth and Gibbs 1990). Even while maintaining legitimacy—especially pragmatic legitimacy, which is subject to shifts in constituencies' self-interest—most organizations operate in environments with multiple, diverse constituencies and ambiguous or changing expectations.

Organizations seeking to manage legitimacy have three basic strategies available to them. first, they can try to change widely shared values and norms to conform to the organization's current practices and procedures. This is difficult for any organization (Dowling and Pfeffer 1975). Second, an organization may choose to adapt to prevailing values and norms. Ashforth and Gibbs

(1990:178) refer to this as substantive management, involving "real, material changes to organizational goals, structures, and processes." Third, an organization may seek "to identify [itself] with legitimate social institutions or practices" (Dowling and Pfeffer 1975). This "symbolic management" is designed to make the organization appear to be consistent with expectations without altering what the organization does (Ashforth and Gibbs 1990).

In the chapters that follow we use the concept of legitimacy to provide a new perspective on union activities. We do this by presenting five cases that show unions engaged in both traditional and nontraditional activities and by using different dimensions of legitimacy—its forms, its management, and the constituencies who confer legitimacy—to analyze these cases.

Legitimacy matters, and an understanding of its role in union activities is useful for both scholars and union officers and staff. For industrial relations scholars, we provide a new lens for viewing the complexity and severity of the unions' dilemma. For union officials and staff, we discuss concepts that they can use to ensure that issues of legitimacy are considered in strategic decision-making as well as everyday union activities. We attempt to discuss legitimacy in a way that appeals to labor activists as well as organizational theorists, to industrial relations scholars and union officers, to supporters and critics of contemporary unions and collective bargaining, and to members of the general public who seek a better understanding of the state of the unions.

Our presentation is straightforward. In chapter 2 we discuss the constituencies who confer legitimacy on unions and the problems of legitimacy faced by unions as a result of having multiple constituencies whose expectations may conflict. In chapters 3 and 4 we present five cases that represent major industrial relations events or issues of the past two decades. Chapter 3 describes three cases that reflect union activities directed at pragmatic and moral legitimacy: the strike at United Parcel Service, an organizing drive at Harvard

University, and the unions' offer of associate membership to non-members. Chapter 4 presents two cases that demonstrate the interplay between pragmatic and moral legitimacy but reveal a more overt effort to gain moral legitimacy: the campaign against NAFTA and the Massachusetts Nursing Association's Safe Care campaign. These cases allow us to assess the management of legitimacy and the different types of legitimacy in unions' attempts to appeal to a wide range of constituencies, including coalition members, the general public, and union members and nonmembers. In the concluding chapter, we review the uses and benefits of the legitimacy perspective, and we ask what legitimacy can tell us about the state of the unions.

CHAPTER 2

Who Confers Legitimacy on Unions?

In this chapter we describe the constituencies that give organizations their legitimacy. Pfeffer and Salancik (1978:194) describe legitimacy as "a conferred status and, therefore, always controlled by those outside the organization." Legitimacy does not necessarily have to be conferred by all of society, or even a large segment of society, but it does need to be conferred by important constituencies on whom the organization depends for its resources and, ultimately, its survival.

Our brief review of industrial relations research dealing specifically with legitimacy, as well as allusions to legitimacy in the popular and research literature, suggests that legitimacy may be conferred (or not conferred, or even withdrawn) by several kinds of groups. We read, for instance, how our system of industrial relations is built on *the public's* conferring legitimacy on unions. Among the public, *nonunion workers* represent a separate and important constituency because they are the source of union growth. On the plant and company levels a crucial union constituency is the *employers,* who accept (or reject) the unions and pave the way to (or strenuously block) labor-management cooperation and employee participation programs. *Coalition partners* are critical constituencies when unions engage in political activities, for without a broad base of support, unions often cannot achieve their political ends. Finally, *members* also have a crucial role; if members do not confer legitimacy on unions, they will be incapable of functioning as organizations, remaining relevant in our society, and compelling employers to deal with them as bargaining agents.

Meyer and Scott (1983:201) ask and then answer a key question about legitimacy: "Whose opinion matters? Those of people who have the capacity to mobilize and confront the organization." Each of these constituencies—the public, nonunion workers, employers, coalition partners, and members—has that capacity, whether it is exercised through employer challenges to unions' rights in the workplace, or members' decision to withdraw their support from or even reject their union. In this chapter we begin with a discussion of each of these different constituencies and conclude with a consideration of how multiple constituencies, as well as changing and conflicting beliefs about what unions should do, make legitimacy problematic.

The General Public

The public is an obvious constituency of labor unions. It is the force behind consumer boycotts in support of strikes and organizing drives and the source of voters for the political candidates and propositions endorsed by unions. Strong public support for unions deters employers from replacing strikers, firing union supporters during organizing drives, or continuing business as usual during strikes.

Despite the importance of the general public as a union constituency, we have only fragmentary and superficial evidence about the legitimacy of unions from the public's perspective. Questions in public opinion polls are too broad, deal mostly with tangential issues, or show mixed results rather than a discernible trend.

On the one hand, there seems to be an undercurrent of support for unions in the most general sense. For example, a 1998 Peter Hart Research poll finds that 34 percent of the public has positive feelings about unions compared to 29 percent with negative feelings ("Public Supports Labor Goals" 1998). A 1999 Gallup Poll shows that by a margin of 65 to 28 percent the public feels that unions help rather than hurt workers. According to other surveys, majorities of respondents believe that unions are strong and good for the country and for workers, and that without unions, laws that help workers would be weakened (Freeman and Rogers 1993; Burkins 1999; Cornfield 1999).

On the other hand, surveys also show a majority believing that unionization arouses management opposition and can thus jeopardize workers' jobs (Freeman and Rogers 1993). The public is evenly split over whether unions help or hurt the economy (Gallup 1997). When they were asked how much confidence they have in various American institutions, survey respondents rated unions near the bottom of the list, followed only by Congress and the criminal justice system ("Gallup/CNN/*USA Today* Poll" 1998). Furthermore, respondents consistently rate union officers low in terms of honesty and ethical practices (Gallup 1997).

The public's support of strikers is also ambiguous. When asked in a 1994 poll conducted by the AFL-CIO whom they would support in a strike, respondents said that they would favor *workers* over employers in a labor dispute by 52 to 17 percent. But they would favor *unions* over employers by only 38 to 30 percent (Meyerson 1998). Apparently, striking workers as individuals or as a group are viewed more favorably than their unions.

To complicate matters further, the public can be fickle. Their opinion of union power (as opposed to unions in general) fluctuates over time and can be shaped by such factors as the frequency of strikes and how much union workers earn compared to nonunion ones. Jarley and Kuruvilla (1994:111) analyzed opinion surveys and concluded:

Unions must walk a fine line in the pursuit of public approval. Unions are popular because they are effective, but in the public's view unions can push their economic gains too far, leading to rising levels of public disapproval. Even the attainment of modest wage gains may bring rising public disapproval if such gains require resort to confrontational tactics.

In sum, survey results show the transitional and uncertain nature of the public's acceptance and support of unions. This becomes more apparent when we look at a key union constituency within the general public: non-unionized workers.

Nonunion Workers

Ninety-seven million workers, or 84 percent of the employed labor force in the United States, are nonunion, that is, not employed at unionized work sites (Burkins 2000). These nonunion workers are the source of union growth, the audience for the appeals of union organizers—and the counterappeals of management. Unions must recruit about a half-million nonunion workers each year just to offset membership losses caused by declining employment in unionized firms (Chaison and Dhavale 1990).

Surveys of nonunion workers are not very useful for appraising their norms and values because, like surveys of the general public, they ask imprecise questions about union support or preference: Do you approve or disapprove of unions? Are unions good for the nation? Would having a union at your workplace help you? Would you support a union if it organized your workplace? How do you rate the honesty and ethical standards of union officers? (Freeman and Rogers 1993; Peter D. Hart Research Associates 1998; Cornfield 1999). In contrast, behavioral studies of the decision of workers to vote for union representation are more revealing. They show a consistent positive relationship between union instrumentality and workers' willingness to support a union in an organizing drive (Deshpande and Fiorito 1989).

We see a strong element of union instrumentality in Brett's (1980) study of unionization, arguably the most common explanation of why workers want unions. Brett proposed that "an employee's initial interest in unionization is based on dissatisfaction with working conditions and the perceived lack of influence to change these conditions" (1980:48). Hence, employers try to diminish the instrumentality of unions by claiming that "working conditions are not so bad, and . . . employees cannot know with certainty what conditions will be like under union representation" (1980:49). "In sum, the employees must decide whether they are willing to take the stand required by collective action and whether they believe that such a stand will help or hurt them" (1980:50). Brett concluded:

> Probably the most important factor accounting for employees' interest in unionization lies in their belief in the *instrumentality* of unions. We found that dissatisfied employees tended not to vote for unionization if they believed the union was unlikely to improve the working conditions that dissatisfied them. On the other hand, even some of the employees who were satisfied with their working conditions voted for union representation because they believed the union was likely to improve conditions. (1980:52, emphasis added)[1]

It should not be implied, however, that workers weigh union instrumentality in an entirely cold, unemotional, and calculating manner. Sometimes strong feelings enter into decisions that are, at their core, pragmatic. This is evident in Kaufman's (1997) explanation of the decision to join a union. He writes, "Part of the decision to seek union representation is instrumental in nature and rests on a pragmatic and largely reasoned calculation of the benefits to be gained versus the costs" (1997:475). But then he adds:

> The motivation to seek a union is greatly enhanced if calculated gain is supplemented or even supplanted by a strong emotional state, be it fear, anger, missionary zeal, or whatever. Emotional in-

tensity can make people persevere in a cause when coldly considered logic would lead them to abandon it, or never embark on it in the first place. (1997:475)

Such emotion is often a product of workers' feeling that something is unfair at the workplace—that what they have achieved in their wages, working conditions, opportunities for promotion, or personal respect has fallen below the level of what they expect and deserve (Kaufman 1997). Undoubtedly, strong feelings would intensify some workers' support of unions during organizing, though the strength and frequency of the emotional element has yet to be estimated. It should be understood, however, that union instrumentality underlies that strong emotional state: first, the workers believe that something very wrong has happened and their treatment by management has been unfair, and second, they believe the union can fix it.

What is perhaps the most serious implication of the instrumentality or pragmatism in union support was captured in a comprehensive, first-of-its-kind survey by Princeton Survey Research Associates, reported by Freeman and Rogers (1994a, b, 1999), which found that workers' preference for union representation declined when they were given a choice of methods that would create less conflict with their employers. About a third of nonunion workers said they would vote for a union to represent them if given the choice. But when asked other questions, workers were revealed to be highly concerned with management attitudes. If given a choice between two hypothetical organizations—"one that management cooperated with in discussing issues, but had no power to make decisions" and "one that had more power, but management opposed"—63 percent of the survey respondents preferred the former (cooperation and no power), and only 22 percent selected more power but with management opposition (Freeman and Rogers 1999:87).

Why were employees so sensitive to management's attitudes about a workplace organization that they preferred a cooperative management to a stronger work organization? The main reason is that most employees believe that management cooperation is essential for any workplace organization to succeed. We asked, "Do you think employee organizations can be effective even if management does not cooperate with them, or do you think they can only be effective if management cooperates?" Three-fourths declared that employee organizations can "only be effective with management cooperation"—four times the percentage who thought management cooperation was not required. (Freeman and Rogers 1999:58)

When pressed further, a majority of the workers said they preferred an organization in which *either* management or workers could raise issues for discussion, in which *both* parties would have to agree on decisions, conflicts would be resolved by an outside neutral party, and employee representatives would volunteer or be elected rather than be chosen by management. They favored an organization independent of management rather than compliant with management, yet they chose one run jointly by management and labor. Their reasons are clear: workers want more influence in workplace decisions and believe they can achieve this through an organization acceptable to management (Freeman and Rogers 1999).

Here we have a common pragmatic perspective. The choice of union representation is evaluated in terms of gains (increasing influence in decisionmaking) without incurring significant costs (arousing employer opposition) (Uchitelle 1994). In other words, "Americans want workplace institutions that will advance their interests in a manner compatible with the goals of the firm" (Freeman and Rogers 1993:34).[2]

Employers

Although it may seem odd to think of employers as a union constituency, unions depend on their decisions and on firms' economic well-being for the employment of members. More important for our discussion, employers have their own expectations about the appropriateness of union representation, and changes in these expectations, as many scholars argue, are behind a recent transformation of labor-management relations.

American managers have never accepted unions as morally appropriate and valued parties to the employment relationship (e.g., Barbash 1987; Carlson 1992; Craypo and Nissen 1993). Their relationship with unions is built on weighing the relative costs and benefits of accepting or avoiding unions. What is to be gained or lost by dealing with unions? And what is to be gained or lost by fighting them?

Strauss (1995:333) observes: "U.S. management has had a long history of fighting unions; in retrospect the period 1940–1980 was only a truce." From the 1940s through the 1970s, employers accommodated unions largely because of the high costs of avoiding them at nonunion facilities or dislodging them at unionized ones (Kochan, Katz, and McKersie 1986). Under the unions' and employers' tacit understandings about their mutual dealings, called the labor accord by industrial relations scholars, unions accepted the right of employers to manage the enterprise within the bounds set by law and collective agreements, and employers accepted the right of unions to exist and negotiate collective agreements. "Management's job is to manage, the union's is to object." that is, to bargain for and police the contract (Strauss 1995:342).

The two agreed to live and let live, though management did reserve the right to oppose unions, within legal bounds, where bargaining relationships were not yet established. The government, seeking to balance the power of workers and management, ensured the right of employees to select their bargaining agents freely and required that the parties bargain with each other in good faith (Adams 1989; Strauss 1995).

Nilsson (1997:334) sees the origins of the accord in the social and political upheavals of the 1930s:

> The bitter battles between labor and management during that era led unions and large corporations to seek out a truce. The truce was greatly facilitated by the passing of the National Labor Relations Act [Wagner Act] which clarified the rules involved in the accord and just as important, established a third party coercive structure [the National Labor Relations Board] to produce and reproduce the accord between labor and management.

For nearly fifty years, labor and management accepted the boundaries between themselves and a way of dealing with each other that they considered, sometimes grudgingly, as fair (Heckscher and Palmer 1993). This was a fundamentally unbalanced relationship, with management serving as a senior partner with largely unrestricted authority to run the enterprise, and the unions as a junior partner with the right to bargain over a narrow range of topics (Gross 1994). Moreover, the accord was never pervasive: it was limited by geography (found mostly in heavily industrialized regions such as the Northeast) and by industry (primarily manufacturing, mining, transportation, and construction). In these regions and sectors, the proportion of the workforce that was unionized was so high that both union and nonunion employers saw little to gain by resisting unions. Wages and working conditions had been effectively taken out of contention (Rogers 1993).

By the late 1970s, the labor accord, where it existed, began to disintegrate. Under intense competitive pressures, management retreated from its commitment to collective bargaining, seeking to repel unions during organizing drives and suppress them at unionized operations (Edwards and Podgursky 1986). Management judged that the costs of dealing with unions had become unacceptably high because of the growth of foreign and domestic nonunion firms and the widening gap between wages and benefits for union versus nonunion workers. Management followed an aggressive market-oriented ideology that justified overtly anti-union activities in the name of achieving the productive flexibility and low labor costs needed for the firm to survive in a highly competitive global economy (Freeman 1989). Gross (1994:51) observed:

> It has become a virtual article of faith that survival (and jobs) in this new era of economic competition depends upon unencumbered and creative management responses to change; the end of high-cost contracts with unions; the retention or regaining of management prerogatives, power, and flexibility; and the freedom to overcome other labor cost advantages enjoyed by competitors.

Because the basis of management's acceptance of unions was pragmatic rather than a deeply felt conviction of the positive role of unions in the society and economy, competitive pressures could cause management to withdraw legitimacy. Employers threw their energy and resources into creating a nonunion environment by displacing unions where they had once accommodated them and reversing earlier union gains in negotiations (Edwards and Podgursky 1986; Nilsson 1997). Rogers (1993:59) concluded that "the elaborate system of rules and understandings, compromise and consent, that had marked U.S. industrial relations for a generation was suddenly transformed." Freeman (1997:25–26) noted the depth of anti-union feelings: "An increasing number of employers seek the 'union-free' environment that only retrograde right-wing ideologues once sought. Many firms that do not espouse the union-free world act as if that was what they truly want when their own work force seeks to organize."

The erosion of the union-management accord in the 1980s manifested itself as intense employer resistance, legal and illegal, to union organizers; tremendous pressure on unions to grant concessions in bargaining; increased management reliance on strikebreakers during bargaining disputes; and a wave of plant closures and relocation of operations to avoid dealing with unions. As early as 1987, Farber (1987:919) was able to characterize such anti-union conduct as "the standard mode of operation in U.S. industry." A decade later, Bronfenbrenner (1998:22) identified employer opposition as the principal force behind the decline in union organizing and found that "employer opposition to organizing is rapidly escalating in scale, sophistication, and effectiveness." And that same year a survey found that "management threats regarding replacement workers [strikebreakers] and plant closings are now a key part of the collective bargaining landscape" (Cutcher-Gershenfeld, Kochan, and Wells 1998: 28).

The accord signified not an ideological acceptance of unionism but a weighing of the gains and losses of dealing with unions rather than repelling them. This pragmatic legitimacy was weak and transitory, as pragmatic legitimacy can often be. Unions faced an onslaught of opposition when many managers could no longer find net value in maintaining their relations with unions.

Coalition Partners

Unions join with organizations in regions or industries to fight plant closures, promote economic recovery, and protect competitive positions (Craypo and Nissen 1993; Nissen 1995). They also join in coalitions to lobby for legislation protecting workers or increasing and extending employee benefits.

Often coalition partners are not traditional allies of unions. For example, the Sierra Club, the national environmentalist group, worked with unions in California in 1998 to defeat a voter initiative that would have prevented unions from using members' dues for political purposes without authorization by the members each year. The environmentalists were concerned about possible curbs on their own use of members' dues ("Sierra Club Opposes Prop. 226" 1998). The Sierra Club's leader in California proclaimed: "When [Proposition 226's supporters] team up to limit democracy, the public should be convinced that although today's target may be working men and women, tomorrow's could be environmental protection and public health" (Craven 1998:1).

In 1999 locals of the United Steelworkers of America, along with those of the United Food and Commercial Workers, the Teamsters, and the Service Employees, joined with a group of environmentalist organizations, including the Sierra Club, to form the Alliance for Sustainable Jobs and the Environment. The Alliance's main purpose was to counter corporate groups that press for changes in environmental and work standards at the meetings of the World Trade Organization. It also demonstrated against employers in labor disputes, helping unions while publicizing employers' activities that endanger the environment and waste natural resources. The objective was to hold employers "accountable for their treatment of the workers and the earth" (Greenhouse 1999c:A12).

Coalitions can also be formed *with* employers, not just against them. In 1998 the Steelworkers joined with several steel companies in a coalition called Stand Up for Steel. Its purpose was to encourage the public to protest and the government to block "the dumping of foreign steel at cutthroat prices" ("Foreign Steel" 1998:A18). The coalition joined organizations that are usually adversaries. During lobbying, high-ranking government officials were met by "union officials and top executives—who rarely find themselves on the same side of the bargaining table" (Sanger 1998:C2).[3]

These coalitions were formed to achieve the desired ends of the coalition partners. Steel company executives and the Sierra Club were not supporting the values inherent in unionism. In contrast, some organizations and individuals form coalitions with unions because they believe they share the same values. Church groups and "concerned citizens' committees" often help unions during strikes and organizing campaigns. They raise funds, encourage strikers, and pressure employers to return to the bargaining table, or not to close their plants or downsize their workforces (Fantasia 1988:180–225; Nissen 1995; Greenhouse 1996b). For example, an association of clergy was essential to a successful nurses' strike at a hospital in Joliet, Illinois. The group was neutral in the formal sense in the strike at a church-affiliated hospital, but it was able to attract public attention to the nurses' campaign, publicizing the nurses' demands in terms of a fundamental right to decent wages, good working conditions, and representation in collective bargaining (Peters and Merrill 1997).[4]

In the mid-1990s a coalition of community groups, including civil rights organizations, helped the Union of Electrical, Radio and Machine Workers negotiate its first collective agreement at Steeltech, a manufacturing firm in Milwaukee. The company had a largely minority workforce, was minority owned, and was created to spur inner-city economic development. The coalition successfully exposed the company's attempt to avoid bargaining with the union. An evaluation of the campaign concluded:

> Political and economic issues provided a sympathetic theme and focus and it would have been difficult, if not impossible, to succeed without them. Nevertheless, few participants raised these themes as the reason for their involvement. Rather, what motivated people was a basic sense of justice, personal contacts with Steeltech workers or their families, and solidarity within the black community around the treatment of workers and the need for jobs. (Sciacchitano 1997:161)

In the years since the mid-1990s, coalitions of unions and clergy and community groups have campaigned for "living wage" ordinances to raise the minimum wage at companies doing business with or receiving tax abatements from city and county governments. Living wage coalitions in forty cities and counties in seventeen states have succeeded in promoting laws affecting 45,000 workers, mostly janitors, security guards, restaurant workers, and school bus drivers. Unions also benefit; these workers occasionally seek union representation, but even when they do not, they no longer provide a low-wage alternative to unionized workers. When unions organize living wage workers, they emphasize that collective bargaining provides continuous benefits, while ordinances can always be reversed if there is a change in legislatures (Uchitelle 1999).

To summarize, some coalition partners, primarily employer groups, lobbying partners, or just organizations with common enemies or fears, confer legitimacy on unions because unions meet instrumental expectations.[5] Others, such as community and clergy groups, confer legitimacy because they see unions as striving for goals that are socially valued and that conform to their norms and values. In this latter instance, coalition partners appear to go beyond pragmatic legitimacy to achieve moral legitimacy. These coalitions have a cohesion based on shared values, not just similar goals; they are more enduring, continuing for example, after an organizing campaign is won or lost, an agreement is negotiated, or a living wage ordinance is passed or defeated. The unions' role in the coalition is not dependent on continued evaluation and approval by coalition partners; it is based on what unions stand for (e.g., protecting poor workers), not what they can contribute to a particular campaign. But even these coalitions can fall apart. The ties between religious groups and labor were strong in the past, particularly during the mass organizing campaigns and union militancy of the 1930s, but alliances dissolved in the 1960s owing to the war in Vietnam (which most unions supported), numerous public charges of union corruption, and unions' apparent indifference to the poor. Alliances were renewed in the late 1990s as unions asserted that their basic goal was justice and fairness for all workers, and as they expanded the intensity and scope of their organizing, seeking in particular to protect lower-paid workers on the margins of the economy (Greenhouse 1999a, b).

Union Members and Covered Nonmembers

So far the constituencies we have mentioned are external to unions. But the unions' key constituency is internal: their members. It may seem incongruous that an organization's main constituency can be part of it, particularly for organizations such as unions, which are self-governing and exist to provide a service—representation—to their members. But members are a constituency because unions have an existence as institutions apart from their members. With their layers of national, regional, and local administrative structures, their numerous officers and administrative and specialist staffs, their assets, investments, and properties, and their constitutions and legal rights and obligations, unions are ongoing institutions—far more than just groups of workers.

Nonetheless, unions are, in the words of Fiorito, Jarley, and Delaney (1993), organizations of, by and for their members. They are *of* members because they are limited to persons with common work interests, that is, with the same or related occupations, industries, or types of workplaces (factories, offices, stores, hospitals, and so on). Unions are *by* workers because most of the effort toward achieving union goals comes from members, whether by serving on committees and in officer positions, walking on picket lines during strikes, or debating union policies at meetings or in workplaces. And unions are *for* members because their purpose is to advance the members' interests by recruiting new members, negotiating and enforcing collective agreements, and supporting political candidates and legislation.

In the most fundamental sense, the 16 million union members in the United States are the unions' lifeblood. They pay dues which are the main source of union revenues. They rise from the rank and file to become officers, moving from part-time to full-time, unpaid to paid, and local to regional or national positions. And because unions are expected to operate democratically, union members participate, through the membership meeting and the ballot, in decisions that range from setting dues and selecting officers to going on strike and ratifying collective agreements. As Masters (1997:63) observed: "Members provide the basic human capital from which unions draw the institutional fiber to exert economic and political influence. The rank and file are an integral source of intellectual and leadership talent as well as the sheer brawn necessary to conduct battle against hostile employers."

It is paradoxical that despite the members' crucial role, most members did not freely choose to join their union. Since the early 1980s about 80 percent of collective bargaining agreements have called for some form of compulsory union membership—requirements that workers join unions as a condition of continued employment or pay agency fees in lieu of joining unions (Delaney 1998). Because there has been so little union organizing over this period, few union members, perhaps less than one in twenty, have actually been part of an organizing campaign or experienced working at their jobs on a nonunion basis (Berger, Olson, and Boudreau 1983).

The fact that most workers did not freely join their unions or select them as their bargaining agents does not mean that they are necessarily dissatisfied. In fact, just the opposite is true. A 1998 survey found that 73 percent of union members had positive feelings about their unions and only 12 percent had negative feelings (the remainder were undecided). Moreover, 46 percent gave unions *very* positive ratings, up from 32 percent the previous year (AFL-CIO 1998). In another survey (Freeman and Rogers 1994a, b, 1999), union members were asked whether they would keep their union or get rid of it if a new election were held today. Ninety percent said they would keep the union.

Underlying these favorable impressions we find pragmatic legitimacy. Members strongly believe that unions are essentially instrumental organizations that are helpful in achieving goals, rather than organizations whose mission and means are socially valued in and of themselves, regardless of their specific outcomes. This is borne out by studies of members' preferences. Freeman and Rogers's (1999) survey, mentioned earlier, found that "current union members . . . overwhelmingly prefer a cooperative management to a powerful workplace organization, but they want to keep the organization they have. . . . A cooperative management and a union would presumably be their ideal world" (1999:59). The reason for this is simple: union members, like nonunion workers, want some form of representation at their workplace but believe they can achieve the most through cooperative and equal dealings with management.

In addition, psychological studies have repeatedly shown positive significant relationships between perceiving that unions would effectively resolve the causes of workplace dissatisfaction and voting for unions in certification elections. After their comprehensive review of behavioral research, Barling, Fullagar, and Kelloway (1992:56) were able to conclude, "There appears to be a consensus in the literature that most workers join unions for instrumental rather than ideological reasons." Members join unions hoping to maximize their self-interest rather than join unions for ideological reasons such as furthering the positive social values of unionism (e.g., helping workers who would have little bargaining power alone, enabling workers to share in decisions that affect them)(Fullagar et al. 1997). But studies have also shown that whenever unions are able somehow to develop ideological bonds with their members, they tend to attract members who are more active and involved than those who rely on instrumental bonds (Heshizer and Lund 1997; Sverke and Sjoberg 1997; Bamberger, Kluger, and Suchard 1999).

This last point is worth emphasizing. The union members' instrumental expectations—that is, their reason for conferring pragmatic legitimacy on unions—cause workers to see themselves as distanced from their unions. As we have found:

It is quite possible ... that most members, never having campaigned for unionism, no longer share their predecessors' or their union officers' sense of mission ... Members may view union representation in narrow instrumental terms, more as an insurance policy or a service to be purchased from an organization than as a worker-controlled organization for empowerment at the workplace or a part of a broader social movement. (Chaison, Bigelow, and Ottensmeyer 1993:150)

Or, as Freeman and Rogers (1994b:33) succinctly described this limited perspective, "Current members appear to see unions as a ticket to a good job with decent pay."

These expectations also shape decision making in unions. The more that members focus on their material gains from union representation, the less they support organizing efforts to extend these gains to nonunion workers. The union must persuade members that organizing increases their own bargaining power by reducing nonunion competition and thus increasing their employers' willingness to agree to the union's terms in negotiations. But this is difficult to do when organizing occurs outside the members' industry or occupation, as it often does now. Hence, union decision makers—officers and staff—are reluctant to divert scarce funds and staff time from representing existing members to recruiting new ones (Chaison and Rose 1991).

As we might expect, judgments about union instrumentality also play a prominent role in the members' decision to decertify their union, that is, to rescind the union's bargaining status and revert to dealing with their employers as individuals without union representation. Reviewing the research literature, Barling, Fullagar, and Kelloway (1992:163) concluded, "The data show that decertification activity is likely if members feel they have been oversold on the benefits the union can provide relative to the costs that will be incurred." They caution unions not to raise members' expectations too high: "It behooves unions to ensure that their members have a realistic understanding of just what benefits the union can achieve." Indeed, the members' evaluation of their union's instrumentality is fairly straightforward, based more on the union's perceived effectiveness than on the members' level of satisfaction with their jobs. While dissatisfied workers may vote to certify a union as a bargaining agent, "dissatisfied individuals who do not perceive the union as *instrumental* in resolving their dissatisfaction will see little use for the union's continued existence. . . . Decertification is more a function of the perceived lack of *instrumentality* of the union than current dissatisfaction" (1992:162, emphasis added).

Finally, it is possible that the definition of union instrumentality is now being modified at firms with profit-sharing or stock option plans. One review observes that "the old lines between labor and capital are becoming blurred as more workers hold stock in their companies and get a cut of corporate profits" and "workers' personal fortunes are dependent on factors such as profits, market share, and stock prices, not just what the union can get at the bargaining table" (Ball, Burkins, and White 1999:A8). When union members focus on the profitability and efficiency of their company, they may begin to evaluate union instrumentality in new ways, not just in terms of collective bargaining outcomes and contract enforcement. They may also see the union as benefiting them by not striking needlessly and causing employers to shift production to nonunion facilities, and by allowing the firm, within the limits of reasonable job and income security, to introduce the new technologies and production processes that help it remain competitive on a global basis.[6]

In addition to their members, unions represent many "freeriders" (people who are covered by collective agreements but who are not union members and do not pay fees to unions) and "cheapriders" (people who are covered by agreements but pay only partial dues, anywhere from 20 to 80 percent of regular dues, to the unions that represent them). We call these people covered nonmembers because they are covered by collective bargaining agreements but have exercised their legal rights under the agreements not to join the union. In 2000 there were about 1.7 million covered nonmembers, or about one of every ten workers represented by unions (Burkins 2000). About half of covered nonmembers pay no dues; the others pay partial dues (called an agency or fair share fee) that cover the costs of representation but not political activity and organizing (Chaison and Dhavale 1992).

Covered nonmembers are an important union constituency because unions are legally obligated to represent them equally and fairly along with members in collective bargaining and when handling grievances about management violations of the collective agreement. But they are less than the equal of union members: covered nonmembers cannot vote in union elections, run for union office, attend union meetings, sit on union committees, or engage in any other union activities. Although covered nonmembers have never been surveyed separately from members, it seems only logical that they are the ultimate pragmatists, seeing their unions in entirely instrumental terms as agents for workplace representation rather than as organizations to join and participate in or as part of a larger movement.

Why Legitimacy Is Problematic for Unions

Legitimacy is always problematic for organizations (Ashforth and Gibbs 1990), and it is especially so for organizations with diverse constituencies. As Meyer and Scott (1983:202) observe, "The legitimacy of a given organization is negatively affected by the number of different authorities sovereign over it and by the diversity or inconsistency of their accounts of how it is to function."

Unions often face situations in which their actions may help them gain or maintain legitimacy with one constituency while jeopardizing it with another. For example, threats to legitimacy can arise when unions stray from the path of bargaining. Union participation in labor-management committees aimed at increasing production and lowering costs might conform to the values of employers (for example, flexible, informal, and cordial dealings with the workers' representative can add value to the firm), but members might see it as co-optation of their union's officers by management and the antithesis of the union's instrumental role as an organization for negotiating at arm's length with employers. Unions have to make a strong case not just to management that the union and its members should play an expanded role in decision making, but to its members that participation did not come at the cost of improved wages and working conditions or the union's ability to enforce the collective agreement (Kochan, Katz, and McKersie 1986).

Coalition activities also provide opportunities for different constituencies to scrutinize the legitimacy of unions. Members may feel that their unions are neglecting their role as workplace representative—the basis for measuring union instrumentality—when they share resources with coalition partners to promote environmental issues or social justice for unemployed or exploited immigrant workers. The public, by contrast, may confer moral legitimacy on unions that work with coalition partners for socially valued objectives rather than acting purely in their members' self-interest.

Conflict may also arise within a single constituency. Within the public and among coalition partners or members, differences can arise that make legitimacy difficult to maintain. For example:

When the Boston teachers' union appealed a court order creating goals for the employment of minority teachers at selective schools, the union may have met the expectations of many members regarding the fulfillment of obligations and the use of the grievance procedure rather than the courts to resolve work assignment disputes. However, its actions may have also conflicted with the values of a significant segment of its membership as well as coalition partners, particularly civil rights organizations. (Chaison, Bigelow, and Ottensmeyer, 1993:148)

The unions' response to affirmative action programs in employment can also bring into play the multiple constituencies and forms of legitimacy. Unions will argue at the bargaining table and in the courts that workers' seniority should be the deciding factor in determining the order of layoffs, promotions, or work assignments. But seniority can have the opposite effect of affirmative action programs, which give preferential treatment in personnel decisions to persons based not on tenure but on their race and gender for the purpose of actively eliminating the vestiges of past discrimination in the workplace. As unions press for seniority, they may strengthen the pragmatic legitimacy that is conferred on them by most of their members but lose it from other members (minorities and women) who gain less from seniority and more from the programs the unions oppose. Unions may also lose moral legitimacy from some coalition partners (e.g., human rights groups) that see them turning their backs on workers suffering from discrimination while their pragmatic legitimacy, conferred by other coalition partners (e.g., groups seeking to restrict foreign trade or block plant closures), is unaffected (Chaison, Bigelow, and Ottensmeyer 1993).

Legitimacy is also problematic for unions because workers (both members and nonmembers), many coalition partners, as well as employers usually gauge the legitimacy of labor unions in instrumental terms. Pragmatic legitimacy is neither powerful nor enduring. It does not elicit members' participation in unions. It does not form a solid foundation for attracting new members, nor lead to lasting, respectful relationships with employers, nor enduring coalitions.

Even when moral legitimacy is conferred by a union's coalition partners, it can be lost over time. We mentioned earlier that, historically, coalition partners were attracted to unions' norms and values and saw unions promoting justice and fairness for everyone and striving to protect the dignity of work. They withdrew that moral legitimacy when unions seemed to follow too narrow an agenda of expanding the gains of their well-off members—a loss that occurred mostly from the 1960s until perhaps the mid-1990s, when unions began a major effort at revitalization. Some coalition partners, most notably the clergy and human rights organizations, now seem to be restoring moral legitimacy to unions, which have begun to resemble their earlier, more militant and socially conscious selves through their pursuit of growth and revival.

Unions look to several constituencies for legitimacy, but the legitimacy they receive is often conflicting, weak, and transitory. Thus, legitimacy is problematic for unions, for it is seldom gained in powerful and lasting ways. But it would be wrong to see unions as passive; unions can and do manage legitimacy, and they can turn it into a significant resource if they prevent or resolve conflicts between the perceptions of different constituencies. In the next two chapters we describe some ways this has been done. We also show how understanding the unions' management of legitimacy gives a fresh perspective on major events in recent industrial relations.

We have intentionally selected cases that represent important trends in industrial relations since the early 1980s: (1) organizing women, clerical workers, and workers in higher education; (2) striking to stop the spread of part-time jobs and the loss of full-time ones; (3) fighting international treaties that increase global trade and threaten unionized jobs in the United States; (4) responding through bargaining and politics to cost cutting and job redesign in the tumultuous health industry; and (5) redefining what a union member is and what unions do.

CHAPTER 3

Managing Pragmatic Legitimacy

In the first two chapters we developed the concept of legitimacy and its value as a conceptual lens for analyzing union activities. In this and the next chapter we turn that lens onto union activities.

We have chosen five cases that reflect both important trends in industrial relations and the interplay of pragmatic and moral legitimacy as unions attempt to develop a foundation that transcends the self-interested calculations of their constituencies. The three cases presented in this chapter illustrate union efforts to gain or maintain pragmatic and moral legitimacy by winning a strike, organizing workers, or extending benefits. The first case, the 1997 strike at United Parcel Service (UPS), was a response to unresolved issues in bargaining with a single employer. This was a classic strike, the result of reaching an impasse over economic issues in negotiations. The second case, the organizing of support staff workers at Harvard University for collective bargaining, reflects a traditional union activity, labor organizing, directed at a nontraditional audience— women in clerical and technical positions in higher education. In these two cases the unions can be understood as providing something of value to constituencies (thereby seeking to maintain and gain pragmatic legitimacy) and as presenting their actions as the right thing to do (thereby seeking to gain moral legitimacy). In the case of the Harvard campaign, the organizers demonstrated that unionism could provide protection and benefits and could do so in a way compatible with socially valued processes and goals. In the case of the UPS strike, the union was able to frame its position in terms that were meaningful to an audience much larger than its membership.

The third case is similar in the interplay of pragmatic and moral legitimacy but very different in terms of outcome. In the late 1980s the AFL-CIO advocated group benefits programs as a way of attracting workers. The effort began with a strong presumption on the part of member unions that it would result in both pragmatic legitimacy (workers would want what the unions offered) and moral legitimacy (offering group benefits was the right, socially valued thing for unions to do). Both presumptions, however, were proved wrong. The juxtaposition of these three cases raises issues about the reinforcing links between pragmatic and moral legitimacy and about the constraints and challenges unions face when they engage in activities that move beyond their traditional boundaries.

The Strike at UPS

The United Parcel strike, like the organizing campaign at Harvard University, was considered a historic turning point for contemporary American labor—proof that unions can succeed in organizing and representing workers on the frontiers of unionism and can deal effectively with large, powerful employers (e.g., Shostak 1991; Kleiman 1997; Witt and Wilson 1999). Striking in support of bargaining demands is a fundamental union activity, and the UPS case illustrates the ability of a union to maintain pragmatic legitimacy with its members while gaining moral legitimacy by transcending parochial concerns and becoming identified with the broader concerns of other constituencies.

In August 1997, 185,000 members of the Teamsters union struck UPS, halting 90 percent of the 12 million packages the company shipped each day. There were two major unresolved issues in bargaining. First, the company wanted to convert the pension plan from a multi-employer arrangement to a single-company one. The

Teamsters called this a greedy pension grab that would cause workers to lose control of their pension fund (Greenhouse 1997b, e). But pensions are complex matters, and the company and employee benefits experts were quick to point out that UPS workers would actually be better off with their own company plan, though this might reduce the benefits to the others remaining under the multiemployer plan (Nagourney 1997; Wolff 1997). Second, the union demanded that the company stop hiring part-time workers and convert part-time jobs into full-time ones. This became the unifying theme of the dispute.

Union victory depended on support from a variety of constituencies: full- and part-time UPS workers and the general public as well as consumers and other unions. UPS would have to give in to the union's demands if it could not continue operations by replacing strikers, if other unions supported the strike with enthusiasm and financial assistance, and if the public refused to ship with UPS or accept the company's deliveries. The Teamsters decided to focus on the part-time issue because it could appeal to a broad range of constituencies and define the strike as a struggle for economic justice. And there was no denying the issue's importance in negotiations: Teamster polls showed that 90 percent of part-timers believed that creating more full-time jobs was important; three-fifths of UPS workers were part-timers (Greenhouse 1997e). But gaining support from other constituencies meant that the impact of part-timers had to be shown in the broadest terms, well beyond the interests of the UPS workers.

The Teamsters characterized the strike as a fight for the rights of all part-timers, not just those at UPS. This was a powerful appeal for two reasons. First, part-timers could attract great sympathy when portrayed as exploited workers bypassed by economic prosperity. Second, their presence aroused the concerns of full-time workers that management might turn full-time jobs into part-time ones to cut labor costs.

At every rally and every press conference before and during the strike, Teamster officers spoke of the plight of the UPS part-timers and linked these workers to underpaid and insecure workers in general (Mitchell 1998), a charge that UPS found difficult to refute. The Teamster president, Ron Carey, saw this as an issue that resonated with the public. His statements emphasized issues that went beyond this particular strike: "America wants to move people from welfare to work but with these low wage part-time jobs, U.P.S. is doing just the opposite" (Greenhouse 1997e:A15); "America doesn't want throwaway workers" (Sonnenfeld 1997:14).

The Teamsters put UPS on the defensive by claiming that the company intended to replace full-time jobs with part-time ones that would not provide workers with sufficient income to support a family. They successfully countered the company's strategy of dividing full-time from part-time employees and continuing operations with the latter.[1] Part-timers saw the Teamsters helping them to become full-time workers, and full-time workers saw their union blocking management's efforts to downgrade their jobs into part-time ones (Greenhouse 1997c, e).

The union also presented the strike in emotional and symbolic terms for the strikers and workers in general as the first battle in the war for part-timers everywhere and as an attack on the emerging contingent economy in which corporations ruthlessly cut costs by replacing expensive full-time workers with cheaper part-timers (Greenhouse 1997a, d; Witt and Wilson 1999). For example, when the strikers received their $55 weekly strike benefits from the Teamsters, an accompanying message read, "Remember: We're fighting not just for Teamster members, but for every working family in America" (Nagourney 1997:8). Their picket signs read, "Part-Time America Doesn't Work" (Sewell 1998:1). A union staff member proclaimed that what was at stake in the dispute was nothing less than "how our society shares prosperity" (Levinson 1997:15). John Sweeney, president of the AFL-CIO, lent his federation's political and financial backing to the strikers: "Because their fight is our fight, we are making this strike our strike" (Levinson 1997:15). He saw the strike as drawing a line between labor and management interests throughout the nation: "This has raised the level of focus on part-time workers and that's why companies that use a lot of part-timers, like Sears Roebuck, have been urging U.P.S. to hang tough" (Greenhouse 1997d:E3). In a television interview, Sweeney presented the strike as a fight against the deterioration of work in America: "Working families all across the country are being squeezed because companies are replacing good paying, full benefit, full-time jobs with low-paying, no benefit, part-time jobs" (Leff 1997:2).

A local Teamster officer in Texas envisioned the strike as a clarion call for action transcending that particular negotiation: "Beyond the issues of the strike, the Teamsters have inspired countless workers from sweatshops to fancy cubicles, from oil fields to physicians. Workers now know that they have options beyond submitting to the unreasonable will of an employer who is not looking out for their well-being" ("Teamsters, Labor Win" 1997:1).

The public sympathized with the strikers because they saw their cause as just. For example, a small business owner, inconvenienced by the late delivery of goods, told a news reporter: "I agree with the Teamsters. UPS has 80 percent of the market. They are a successful company, and they can afford to pay full-time jobs. Those workers work hard and they deserve full-time pay and full-time benefits" (Greenhouse 1997d:A1). The plight of part-timers contrasted with the booming economy; some workers were clearly not sharing in the prosperity, and others were finding their jobs threatened by a profitable and exploitive employer (Heath 1998). There seemed to be a contradiction between the financial condition of UPS and that of its newly hired workers. For instance, one observer pointed out:

In the last half decade, UPS has doubled its profits to over one billion dollars annually, while four out of every five jobs it has created have been part-time with a wage nearly identical to that offered in the early 1980s. This mirrors the American economy on the whole, which has experienced stagnant and declining real wages despite record growth. (Wolff 1997:81)[2]

A Gallup Poll conducted midway through the strike showed that 55 percent of the public supported the strikers and 27 percent backed the company (Nagourney 1997).

After two weeks, a settlement was reached that analysts found to be much more favorable to the union than to management. The company accepted the union's demand to make ten thousand part-time workers full-time, but over five years, not four years as demanded by the union.[3] Management's demands for a company-based pension plan were abandoned. Union leaders hailed the strike as a great victory not just for UPS workers but for all workers because it addressed the need for good jobs (Greenhouse 1997c). Ron Carey proclaimed it to be nothing less than "a victory over corporate greed" (Sewell 1998:1) and "an historic turning point for working people in this country (Schlesinger and Wysocki 1997:A1). John Sweeney of the AFL-CIO called it "a wake-up call for corporate America and a reversal of years of unions decline" (Baker 1997:1).[4]

By focusing the strike simultaneously on two aspects of alleged management power and selfishness—the condition of part-time workers and the threat to full-time work posed by part-time work—the Teamsters' campaign offered concrete outcomes that met the needs of both full- and part-time strikers (thus maintaining pragmatic legitimacy with its members). It was also perceived as doing the right thing not only by the strikers but also by the labor movement and the public in general, thus gaining moral legitimacy. Pragmatic legitimacy was conferred on the union because it was seen as being responsive to the job security concerns of a large number of workers—both members and nonmembers. The strike was directed at achieving contract language that would convert part-time to full-time jobs, a tangible objective widely hailed by both full-time and part-time workers, the labor movement in general, and the public (McMurdy 1997). The union was able to gain moral legitimacy by successfully casting the strike in broad terms that suggested the promotion of societal welfare, that is, part-time workers are not adequately protected and should be, and full-time workers' jobs should be secure. To some degree the strike lent moral legitimacy to the entire union movement. As a top AFL-CIO officer observed, "The UPS strike showed the public that unions are in tune with what people really care about", (AFL-CIO executive vice president Linda Chavez-Thompson, quoted in Kleiman 1997:sec. 6, p. 1). A major union was showing that its concerns were those of the greater society and that it was willing to confront a powerful company to promote those concerns.[5]

The Organizing Campaign at Harvard University

When the Harvard Union of Clerical and Technical Workers (HUCTW) began organizing the 3,600 support staff workers (secretaries, library assistants, laboratory assistants, accounting clerks, and so on) at Harvard University, it found that the vast majority were proud to work for a prestigious institution and were unsure if collective bargaining was appropriate in such an academic workplace. Indeed, two previous efforts by other unions to win certification elections in 1977 and 1981 were unsuccessful. Looked at in the context of legitimacy, the previous efforts had focused solely on pragmatic legitimacy and had failed to address workers' concerns. In this instance, however, the union was able to win a certification election by identifying with the values held by the workers and thus gaining both pragmatic and moral legitimacy. They skillfully communicated to workers that joining a union would not just advance their self-interests but would improve Harvard as an educational and research institution. The campaign coalesced around the slogan "It's not anti-Harvard to be pro-union."

HUCTW organizers praised Harvard's excellence while claiming that it would be even better if its workers were given a collective voice. The union would not bring Harvard to its knees but would bring it to its senses.

The objective of organizing, Harvard workers were told, would be to achieve negotiations to establish a system for their participation in decision making. Rather than focusing on a specific benefit to be sought in collective bargaining, the organizers pointed to the goal of achieving power through participation. They were careful not to specify the structure of the local union or overemphasize what HUCTW would negotiate for once certified. They simply promised to open doors—to give workers access, for the first time, to the decision-making processes at the university (Weinstein 1988; Oppenheim 1991; Hurd 1993; Savage 1996; Hoerr 1997).

The HUCTW organizers also campaigned in a manner designed to appeal to support staff who were mostly women (83 percent) and employed in a decentralized setting—four hundred buildings and two thousand work sites throughout the Boston area. Believing that these workers shared a strong inclination to relate to one another through social and work networks, the union adopted and refined a system of one-on-one organizing with continuous meetings between individual workers and organizers (who were also workers). Organizers seldom used campaign literature or group meetings, the two mainstays of traditional organizing in industrial firms and the earlier campaigns at Harvard. Rather, by relying on individual, personal contacts, they created a sense of community among the dispersed Harvard staff and dispelled workers' initial beliefs that the union was an organization apart from themselves. This proved to be an effective strategy for organizing the many women workers at Harvard who felt patronized by the university administration and excluded from decision making yet were uncertain whether an external organization could produce anything more than conflict with the administration (Savage 1996; Hoerr 1997). But at the same time, the campaign was careful to address some serious economic concerns: the Harvard workers' low pay, their limited opportunities for promotion, and their need for affordable day care and improved health care and pension plans (Hurd 1993).

HUCTW carefully distanced itself from conventional labor unions and their assumptions that relations with employers must be adversarial and directed by a knowledgeable and experienced union hierarchy. In contrast, the organizers identified most closely with the values of the women's movement, including the need for a sense of community among marginalized workers, an emphasis on power sharing through participation based on knowledge and mutual respect, and the recruitment of supporters through a network of one-on-one contacts among persons with shared values and concerns ("Finding Their Voice" 1993; Savage 1996). Chris Rondeau, the coordinator of the campaign, remarked that young female workers at Harvard were particularly energized "because, for them, the unionization experience is an extension of the political fight for women's recognition in general" (quoted in Shostak 1991:97).

According to one study, the two earlier organizing campaigns at Harvard failed because their structures, processes, and assumptions were not congruent with the values and expectations of support staff members. The organizers relied on campaign literature rather than personal contacts; they created the impression that they were organizing on behalf of the national union rather than the workers; they organized against the boss rather than for the workers (favoring a highly adversarial approach with critical attacks on the university's values, policies, and administrators); and they focused on narrow issues rather than the power of self-representation (Hoerr 1997). The HUCTW campaign succeeded by following simple principles: "Don't organize against the boss. Don't organize around issues. Don't organize against the institution." ("Finding Their Voice" 1993:2).

The organizing campaign established the union's moral legitimacy on two levels: as an organization to help rather than punish

Harvard by giving its workers a collective voice, and as a community of workers that connects rather than directs them. It did far more than provide information about the benefits and protections of collective bargaining. Organizers knew that a purely informational campaign would have been another organizing failure. They focused on both the "head and heart," believing it essential that workers have an emotional connection to the union and to one another as union members rather than only a knowledge of what the union might accomplish (Oppenheim 1991). Subsequently, the organizers applied their approach to successful campaigns among the support staff at the University of Minnesota, the University of Illinois, and the University of Massachusetts Medical Center.

In its first round of negotiations with the university, HUCTWU continued to emphasize membership participation. Transitional teams of management and workers held meetings prior to formal negotiations to establish the boundaries and tenor of bargaining. Separate bargaining tables were used for discussions of issues ranging from salary structure to mutual respect and cooperation between the union and management. Lawyers were barred from negotiations because of their adversarial and technical perspectives.

After five months, the union and the employer reached an agreement that not only produced substantial improvements in wages and benefits (e.g., a 32.5 percent salary increase over three years and significantly better health care and maternity leave plans), but also formed joint labor-management teams to define and enforce work rules that would otherwise have been covered in technical clauses of collective agreements. Both management and the union praised the agreement's participative features, though union members seemed most impressed by the gains in wages and benefits (Weinstein 1988; Hurd 1993). A collective agreement extending through June 2001 was ratified by 82 percent of the members in March 1998. It included salary increases and additional family leave provisions as well as a continuation of the structures and policies for participation ("HUCTW Ratifies Agreement to Extend Contract" 1998).

The campaign at Harvard became legendary. It was widely hailed by the popular press and the labor movement as proof that unions could appeal to workers once considered beyond the scope of collective bargaining (Hurd 1993). It seemed to signal a new life for the labor movement after years of continuing decline. Although it was undoubtedly innovative in approach (e.g., in its strong reliance on personal contacts and its refusal to attack the employer overtly), the Harvard campaign was nonetheless conventional in many respects. HUCTW presented itself as a labor union (although a nontraditional one), collected membership cards and petitioned for a certification election, and sought to represent workers at their workplace through collective bargaining with their employer.

Indeed, at its core the Harvard campaign was classic unionism. It emphasized the strength of the collective, the common goals and magnified power of a community of workers, the gains for individuals working not alone but as members of a bargaining unit. It sought to convey a sense of "dignity, fairness, respect and participation" (Harvard Union of Clerical and Technical Workers n.d.:2). In this way, HUCTW carefully and consistently presented a vision of union representation that was compatible with the values of workers with little prior experience of or faith in unionism. But at the same time, it emphasized the economic gains possible with unionism but lacking at Harvard without it (hence the popular slogan "You can't eat prestige").

This case illustrates the important role that moral legitimacy can play even in attempts to gain pragmatic legitimacy. It was not sufficient to cater entirely to the self-interests of the workers. The union also had to show that its goals were consistent with valued social goals, in this instance equality, community, empowerment, and participation.

Associate Membership and Group Benefits Programs

In 1985 an AFL-CIO strategy committee published a ground-breaking report titled *The Changing Situation of Workers and Their Unions*. As a series of recommendations about how the federation and its affiliates should respond to the changing workforce, the report became the blueprint for efforts to reinvigorate the union movement and expand the strength and scope of union representation (Perl 1985; McDonald 1987). Among its conclusions, the strategy committee (the AFL-CIO Committee on the Evolution of Work) observed that many workers wanted to "forward their interests in ways other than what they view as the traditional form of union representation—in their view, an adversarial collective bargaining relationship" (AFL-CIO 1985:18). The committee encouraged affiliated unions to explore new ways of representing workers if they were unable to negotiate collective agreements with their employers:

> New categories of membership should be created by individual unions or on a federation-wide basis to accommodate individuals who are not part of organized bargaining units, and affiliates should consider dropping any existing barriers to an individual's retaining his membership after leaving an organized unit. (AFL-CIO 1985:19)

Those in the new categories would be known as associate members. The advocates of associate membership programs sought to do nothing less than redefine how workers can join unions and be represented by them.

In this case study we briefly review and evaluate the most basic approach to associate membership: the provision of group benefits to a new category of union members. As a plan to forward workers' interests, it sought to gain pragmatic legitimacy for the unions. But it also sought to gain moral legitimacy as it identified group benefits with traditional union values. Union efforts, however, were not successful on either score.

Benefits programs for associate members were negotiated with providers (e.g., insurance companies, banks, health care agencies) and offered by the Union Privilege Benefits Corporation, a not-for-profit organization created by the AFL-CIO in 1986. The federation set up Union Privilege to achieve "collective purchasing power in the marketplace" for regular and associate union members (Kirkland 1987:1). Its benefits included low-fee and low-interest credit cards, legal aid services, and life insurance. Union leaders hoped that providing these benefits to associate members paying less than regular dues would prove attractive to the 28 million former union members still in the workforce, the 30 million workers who responded in opinion surveys that they wanted to join a union but did not have one at their workplace, and the hundreds of thousands of workers who voted for unions during organizing campaigns that the unions lost (McDonald 1987).

The group benefits approach focuses almost exclusively on consumer interests by enrolling workers who want to increase their personal welfare and gain access to "cut-rate consumer service with no need to subordinate [their] own interests to those of a work group" (Jarley and Fiorito 1990:212).[6] Several unions offered programs, but the results were disappointing. For example, the American Federation of Teachers (AFT) created a statewide organization, the Texas Federation of Teachers–Professional Educators Group, to which it could affiliate associate members. Using a major advertising firm, the AFT launched a direct-mail campaign to recruit the 147,000 teachers in the state who were not union members or were members of the rival National Education Association. Associate members were not allowed to vote in AFT elections but received group insurance and discounts on legal assistance, prescriptions, and travel. The cost of associate membership was $50 per year, a quarter of the cost of regular AFT dues. Of the teachers who were contacted, only 20,000 (about 14 percent of the total) requested more information. Only 976 teachers (5 percent of respondents) joined as associate members. The cost of the campaign was nearly $1 million, or over $1,000 for each new member—more than the cost of traditional organizing for collective bargaining in the public sector. The AFT justified this expense by claiming that the responses helped it pinpoint clusters of union supporters in Texas and enabled it subsequently to launch organizing campaigns for regular bargaining relationships (Tasini 1986).

A survey conducted by Fiorito and Jarley (1992) uncovered twenty associate membership programs, of which eighteen were formed after the AFL-CIO's 1985 report. There was great variety in the programs in terms of the rights of associate members and the benefits offered to them,[7] but the programs were generally disappointing as a way to jump-start union growth and broaden the scope of union representation. One critic saw a certain irony in the limited attractiveness of the group benefits programs:

> The associate membership campaign has been a great success but not to the audience that it was supposed to be directed. *Union members* have responded in large numbers to the offers of no-fee credit cards, medical plans, travel agent services, legal assistance, and other benefits provided by the program, but nonunion employee recruitment has apparently been minor, especially in the private sector. These benefits are already available to most such employees from their employers, or from other sources. (Northrup 1991:334–335, emphasis added)

Moreover, an analysis found that a majority of former union members thought group benefits were attractive, but they did not care who offered the benefits (Wilson Center, 1992). They were equally likely to enroll whether the sponsoring organization was a bank, an insurance company, a buying club, or a labor union.

As an alternative to representation through collective bargaining, associate membership fared poorly. Surveys administered during selected organizing campaigns found that even when unions did not enjoy majority support, traditional union representation was favored by nearly a 6-to-1 margin over associate membership with group benefits (34 percent to 6 percent). This was true despite the low cost of the plans relative to the benefits they provided. Significantly, the plans appealed least to those workers who considered themselves pro-union. During interviews "many union adherents said that the associate membership approach was not related to their needs on the job, nor to their reasons for wanting a union" (Wilson Center 1992:7). A review of surveys concluded: "The weak appeal . . . of the associate membership concept as a 'stand alone' alternative to traditional collective representation is a testament to the importance workers attach to the basic functions of unions [i.e., collective bargaining, grievance handling, and lobbying for labor legislation]" (Wilson Center 1992:7).

The appeal of group benefits did not rest solely on pragmatic grounds. Proponents of group benefits programs also tried to make a case that what they sought was entirely compatible with traditional unionism: the provision of group benefits was actually "a return to the 100-year-old roots of organized labor, when the prime tangible benefit of union membership had little to do with collective bargaining and unions functioned primarily as mutual aid societies for workers" (McDonald 1987:227).[8] And, they argued, these links with the past had never been completely severed. Associate membership status through group benefits continued in some unions (e.g., the American Federation of Teachers and the Amalgamated Clothing and Textile Workers) as a way to remain in contact with retired members or with workers who had supported the unions during unsuccessful organizing drives.

But for many in the labor movement, group benefits programs seemed a radical departure from the usual *modus operandi* of unions. Labor unions, they argued, are bargaining agents, pure and simple, that negotiate collective agreements for members and enforce them in the workplace. The unions' members and officers and the broader labor movement expect—many even demand—that unions conform to their bargaining role. Associate membership seemed to draw unions into uncharted waters not just by establishing a new category of membership but by redefining the unions' mission in terms of individual members: "Whereas traditional membership stresses a union's role as a bargaining agent, associate membership stresses national unions' providing benefits directly to members" (Fiorito and Jarley 1992:1070).

Also, to many, recruiting associate members meant "organizing on the cheap," providing watered-down unionism, and growing the labor movement but without instilling worker solidarity, confronting hostile employers, and negotiating collective agreements. The pursuit of associate members seemed a sign of the unions' weakness and their shirking of the tough work of organizing. In a typical biting comment, one union officer dismissed associate members, saying, "We think we can organize real members, not play members" ("Labor Letter" 1991:1).[9]

At present, little is heard in the popular press or academic literature about associate membership. It has become a low priority for union and federation leadership (Stone and Gallagher 1997), in stark contrast to the excitement following its introduction in the late 1980s. Essentially, the provision of group benefits for associate members did not meet the expectations of union officers and current and potential members about what was appropriate for unions to do. It did not evolve as an alternative form of union membership (Lawler 1990).[10] It was highly unlikely that unions would gain moral legitimacy by offering group benefits to such members. There was only a faint ideological connection between group benefits programs and the values and principles associated with unionism, and this was through historical reference to the pre–collective bargaining activities of the earliest labor unions.

Suchman (1995) observes that a hospital would lose moral legitimacy if it performed exorcisms, even if all of the patients recovered, because exorcisms fall outside the realm of socially accepted techniques and procedures for hospitals. While certainly not akin to exorcism, group benefits programs for associate members did fall outside the realm of techniques and procedures considered acceptable for unions by their constituencies. Moral legitimacy was thus not conferred by constituencies, and pragmatic legitimacy was weak at best.

Three Cases: A Comparison

Comparing the three cases discussed in this chapter in terms of constituencies, management of legitimacy, and the forms of legitimacy highlights a number of similarities and differences among them. They clearly differ as to constituencies and, to a lesser extent, the management of legitimacy. All three, however, demonstrate the importance of moral legitimacy to a union's ability to gain pragmatic legitimacy. In each case, a union was seeking to serve the self-interest of some constituency: the UPS strikers, the workforce at Harvard, or individuals seeking inexpensive benefits. But they could not gain pragmatic legitimacy unless their actions were also seen as right and proper. Thus, the cases in this chapter illustrate the pitfalls as well as the challenges that the need for moral legitimacy creates.

As we have seen, the constituencies differed among the cases. At Harvard, the primary constituency was the workforce the union sought to organize. The employer played only an indirect role, although the union had to be sensitive to the value the workers placed on Harvard as an institution. The UPS case demonstrates the role not only of members but also of constituencies in the wider society—the general public and consumers in particular. The strike could not have been successful without an appeal that extended beyond the strikers. In the case of group benefits for associate members, the intended constituencies were former union members and nonmembers. The option, however, had limited appeal and failed to add significant numbers of associate members to union rolls.

In terms of the management of legitimacy, there are many similarities. In each instance the union sought to gain legitimacy, whether with the public or with nonmembers. The specific strategies, however, differed. The Teamsters' effort can be understood as an attempt to identify the strike with widely shared values that transcended the concerns of workers at UPS. Framing the strike as a struggle for the rights of all part-timers and the simultaneous protection of full-timers had an appeal that extended considerably beyond UPS. The strategies used by the union organizers at Harvard can be interpreted as an organization managing legitimacy by adapting its "methods of operation to conform to prevailing definitions of legitimacy" (Dowling and Pfeffer 1975:127). They adapted the form and content of their campaign to appeal to a support staff, mostly women, employed in a decentralized setting, who took pride in working for a prestigious institution.

Looked at in the context of managing legitimacy, unions offering associate membership through group benefits may be either trying to change norms and expectations about what unions do or identifying the new with the old, that is, linking the provision of group benefits to traditional unionism (as they hope to define it). But as the unions tried to operate in nontraditional contexts—taking on new activities and appealing to new types of audiences—beliefs about what unions *should* do constrained what they *could* do. The group benefits program for associate members was individual- and consumer-oriented. As such, it was widely criticized within the labor movement for deviating from the collectivist principles and workplace orientation that underlie traditional union activities. Perhaps an automobile manufacturer or retail store can operate in a nontraditional context, for example, by diversifying into financial and other benefits programs for consumers. But the fundamental and deeply embedded premise of unionism—that the unions' role is to act as a counterbalance to the power of employers by negotiating collective agreements—means that unions cannot diversify without impunity.

The challenge for unions that these cases illustrate is how to manage legitimacy, first, by pursuing both moral and pragmatic legitimacy, and second, by letting the former strengthen the latter. Pragmatic legitimacy alone forms an unstable base in any context—constituencies' approval of means and ends can be fleeting—and serving self-interests may not be sufficient for institutional growth and survival. To gain pragmatic legitimacy with new constituencies or to maintain it with traditional ones, unions also need to gain moral legitimacy.

The UPS strike shows a union engaged in a basic union activity, one that for the strikers had both pragmatic legitimacy (it was designed to get them improved benefits and working conditions) and moral legitimacy (striking to protect good—that is, full-time—jobs and against an uncaring and greedy employer). But to be effective it required support from consumers and the public—a public that did not benefit directly from the strike (in fact, some were inconvenienced) and could not be assumed to embrace strikes as an inherently worthy activity. The outcome of the strike, framed in terms of helping exploited part-time workers, was important to other constituencies (the public) not because it would have an immediate benefit but because it had moral legitimacy. The interplay between pragmatic and moral legitimacy is particularly noteworthy here because it demonstrates unions' need for a base that extends beyond the narrow self-interests of members. That wider base may often be necessary for a strike to garner support and to succeed against a large and resource-rich employer.

At Harvard, the interplay between pragmatic and moral legitimacy was more obvious. Organizers sought to achieve both by introducing innovations in union representation to appeal to a workforce that was nontraditional for unions. Promoting the self-interested calculations of the support staff at Harvard would not have been sufficient for union victory. There had to be a sense of community, social purpose, participation, and empowerment of marginalized workers—all factors underlying moral legitimacy, the belief that unionism is right. This was not an easy task—the margin of victory in the certification election at Harvard was less than 1 percent—but it was not an impossible task because moral legitimacy was used to gain pragmatic legitimacy.

The advocates of the group benefits programs for associate union members implicitly assumed that moral legitimacy would somehow be automatically conferred on their efforts. They seemed to expect that the target audience would not only value what unions could do for them but also see it as the right thing to do and a modern-day continuation of the early mission of unions. They also assumed that the unions themselves would be enthralled by the possibilities of quick membership gains, however gotten. But pragmatic legitimacy was being sought by offering a benefit without a firm ideological basis, without a sense of doing anything other than providing services for a fee. The proponents of the plans emphasized that good benefits (e.g., credit cards, group discounts) could be had at good rates—an appeal to consumerism—but they neglected to focus on other aspects of the program such as work-related counseling and protection. The campaign seemed nothing but a marketing exercise, not a return to the roots of unionism by expanding the boundaries of accepted union activities.

We concluded in chapter 2 that one reason why legitimacy is problematic for unions is that constituencies primarily confer pragmatic legitimacy. In two of the cases—the UPS strike and organizing at Harvard—we see unions gaining or maintaining pragmatic legitimacy by also seeking moral legitimacy. In the third case, group benefits, we see the constraints under which unions operate when they attempt to move beyond the bounds of traditional activities. Many within the labor movement, as well as nonunion workers, believe that nontraditional activities such as providing group benefits fall outside the realm of activities encompassed by pragmatic legitimacy. For unions to enter the scope of pragmatic legitimacy, nontraditional activities have to be somehow linked to traditional practices of union organizing and collective bargaining.

Finally, because moral legitimacy is weak or nonexistent for unions, constituencies are not able to confer pragmatic legitimacy unquestioningly. If unions are not widely perceived as socially valued institutions, their instrumentality is more apt to be judged by constituencies on a continuous cost-benefit basis and rejected. Pragmatic legitimacy cannot be assumed in the absence of a shared view of the moral legitimacy of unions.

CHAPTER 4

Gaining Moral Legitimacy

Like those in the previous chapter, the cases presented here show the interplay of pragmatic and moral legitimacy as unions seek to gain and maintain legitimacy with different constituencies. The difference is in the scope of their efforts. With UPS, Harvard, and the associate membership campaign, unions were engaging in very specific activities that were intended to provide specific outcomes of value to members or nonmembers. In the next two cases unions were also seeking to protect and provide services to members, but their efforts encompassed a broader agenda—the promotion of political goals—and they emphasized social welfare. As a result, the concept of moral legitimacy assumes a more central role in these cases, for it reflects "beliefs about whether [an] activity effectively promotes social welfare [and] a prosocial logic that differs fundamentally from narrow self-interest" (Suchman 1995:579).

The two cases—the campaign against the North American Free Trade Agreement (NAFTA) and the activities of the Massachusetts Nurses Association (MNA)—show unions joining in a common front and promoting issues that had a broad appeal yet were also consonant with efforts to save jobs. The NAFTA campaign was conducted at the highest level—it sought to shape national trade policy—and it was far removed from the kind of organizing and negotiating activities with which unions are closely associated. No single company or even industry was targeted in the campaign, nor was the objective to unionize workers or represent them in dealings with their employers. Rather the unions fought NAFTA because they believed it would have a disastrous impact on these activities. The unions worked closely in coalitions with other groups as they sought, unsuccessfully, to block the passage of the pact.

In the MNA's Statewide Campaign for Safe Care, the union's activities included developing and lobbying for a legislative package as well as organizing and negotiating in reaction to a systemic problem in the state's health care system. Through coalitions and media exposure, the union linked nurse staffing with patient safety, simultaneously promoting the interests of its members and the concerns of the general public.

The Campaign against NAFTA

American unions opposed NAFTA because they believed it encouraged companies to transfer production to Mexico and thus failed to promote American economic and social interests.[1] It would, the unions argued, create massive job losses in the United States through plant relocation, depress the wages and purchasing power of American workers, and severely weaken existing trade laws. All this would occur without proper environmental safeguards in Mexico or assurances that the wages and working conditions of Mexican workers would improve. The unions conceded that trade agreements are useful if they improve the lives of each nation's citizens, but they saw NAFTA as an unbalanced agreement designed to promote and protect the interests of company owners and managers (Labor Advisory Committee 1992: AFL-CIO Task Force on Trade 1993; Housman and Orbuch 1993; Donahue 1993b).

The NAFTA case illustrates two related ways of managing legitimacy, both of which sought to identify unions with widely shared values: unions joined a common front in opposition to NAFTA, and they consistently emphasized themes that transcended parochial goals. By finding common ground with members of a diverse coalition and aligning with goals that widened the basis of their opposition to the trade pact, unions were able to lead the campaign against NAFTA and enhance their moral legitimacy as a voice not just for members but for workers in general.

The Anti-NAFTA Coalition

NAFTA was signed by the leaders of the United States, Canada, and Mexico on December 17, 1992, passed by the House of Representatives on November 17, 1993, and the Senate on November 20, and went into effect on January 1, 1994.[2] It was the most comprehensive free trade pact ever negotiated among regional trading partners short of the European common market and widely considered to be a major step toward free trade throughout the Western Hemisphere (Hufbauer and Schott 1993). The agreement progressively eliminated nearly all U.S.-Mexico tariffs over a ten-year period, except for a few tariffs for trade-sensitive industries (e.g., agriculture, textiles, and apparel), which were to be phased out over fifteen years. Mexico-Canada tariffs would be phased out over ten years.

NAFTA was intended to protect foreign investors and their investments in the free trade area against discriminatory treatment, burdensome government regulations, and unfair expropriation of assets. It guaranteed service providers equal treatment in the NAFTA countries, and it continued the tariff reductions of the free trade agreement between the United States and Canada passed in 1988 (U.S. General Accounting Office 1993a, b).

The pro-NAFTA lobby, USA*NAFTA, claimed that the pact would create twice as many jobs as it eliminated; enable Mexico to confront its pollution problems successfully; encourage economic development in Mexico, thus reducing the flow of illegal immigrants into the United States; and create new markets for American goods and services. NAFTA, they argued, would benefit all Americans by allowing U.S. companies to play on their competitive strengths in an open marketplace (e.g., Behr 1993c; Council of the Americas 1993; Purcell 1993).

In May 1991 fast track negotiating authority for the president (giving the President power to negotiate agreements that Congress could vote up or down but not amend) was approved by Congress. The campaign against the passage of NAFTA was carried out between that date and November 1993, when the House of Representatives and the Senate passed the bill.

NAFTA was fought by a wide-ranging and loosely formed alliance, what one observer called "an ideologically chaotic group; from columnist Patrick J. Buchanan on the right to Texas billionaire Ross Perot in an undefined center to Ralph Nader on the consumer movement left. Individuals and groups associated with the liberal wing of the Democratic Party, particularly organized labor, were the dominant forces" (Edsall 1993:A39). At the center of this alliance was the NAFTA Fair Trade Campaign, a group composed of the AFL-CIO and its affiliated unions, and of several human rights, environmental, anti-poverty, consumer protection, religious, womens', farmers', students', and public policy organizations (Robinson 1994).

In the past, the unions had a strained relationship with the other groups in the anti-NAFTA coalition. Environmentalists and unions had clashed over the damage caused by manufacturing and development. Human rights organizations often failed to include the workers' right to unionize in their agendas (Behr 1993b). Since the late 1980s, however, unions had worked together with many of these organizations to oppose other trade agreements, the spread of *maquiladora* plants (plants set up by American firms in Mexico that do not pay tariffs for products assembled and shipped to the United States), and the fast track authority for presidents to negotiate trade pacts. Unlike those issues, NAFTA had great public visibility.

In their opposition to NAFTA, the unions joined with other organizations united in their belief that the trade pact would "help multinational companies and hurt the little guy" (Davis 1992:A1), but which looked at NAFTA's implications from different perspectives. The environmentalists, for example, believed that NAFTA would not meet the minimal environmental standard of "no more harm to the environment through trade agreements," and that NAFTA would weaken environmental laws and produce unsafe conditions at Mexican plants and in neighboring communities on both sides of the border (Audley 1993). Religious organizations such as the United Methodist Church were concerned about the social consequences of the deteriorating living conditions of Mexican workers and job losses in the United States (Davis 1992).

The unions' incorporation of the interests of other groups was apparent in the broad framework of a conference on trade, Trade for the Twenty-first Century (September 8–10, 1992), jointly sponsored by the AFL-CIO, the Sierra Club (the nation's largest environmental organization), the Friends of the Earth (a global environmental advocacy group), the Farmers Union (a national organization of farm families promoting cooperation, education, and legislation), and Public Citizen (a consumer research and lobbying organization founded by Ralph Nader). In a fact sheet accompanying the conference program, the AFL-CIO mentioned its concerns along with those of the other sponsors:

> [The proposed trade pacts] would serve to increase unemployment in vital sectors of the economy; erode the nation's industrial base; jeopardize our efforts for a cleaner environment and a safe food supply; harm the nation's farmers; encourage corporations to invest overseas, instead of in the United States; seriously weaken existing trade remedy and "Buy America" laws; and compromise our system of democratic decision-making. (AFL-CIO 1992:1)

Five Themes

Unions presented a broad appeal that emphasized—in congressional testimony, debates, promotional literature, interviews with the media, position papers, and press releases—five principal themes. These themes transcended protecting the interests of members and encompassed the interests of other constituencies.

1. *Trade is not only a labor issue but an environmental one as well.* Environmental harm was a unifying concern of the coalition against NAFTA and a continuation of many of the opponents' earlier objections to unregulated trade and industrial expansion. The unions already had a track record of activism on environmental issues along the Mexican border prior to the NAFTA campaign. For example, in 1989 the AFL-CIO published a report, *The Maquiladoras and Toxics: The Hidden Costs of Production South of the Border* (Kochan 1989). This study, prepared by Leslie Kochan, a specialist in environmental policy, showed not only that *maquiladoras* cost Americans their jobs as employers closed plants and moved across the Rio Grande, but also that these facilities released toxins into the water, air, and land. The side effects ranged from polluted water supplies and irrigation waters near the *maquiladoras* to the lack of basic safety and health protection for the workers at those plants. The unions took up this theme and found common ground with coalition partners by arguing that the environmental damage that followed the spread of the *maquiladoras* would become the norm throughout Mexico if NAFTA were passed (Davis 1992).

2. *NAFTA would affect the fundamental economic and social well-being of all Americans.* NAFTA was characterized not as a typical cross-border trade agreement but as an investment agreement intended to enable companies to shift production to Mexico and take advantage of the poverty of Mexican workers (Behr 1993a). The unions' opposition to NAFTA was presented as a fight for social and economic justice rather than just a campaign to protect their members' jobs from the forces of global competition. For example, an AFL-CIO handbook for lobbying and media relations instructed union officers to respond to the question "Aren't unions just trying to hold on to a dwindling membership?" by stating:

NAFTA will affect workers in every industry—union members and non-members—and in every sector of the economy. That's why we're working with allies in a number of groups—the National Farmers Union, Sierra Club, Public Citizen and others. From auto plants to food processing firms like Birdseye and Green Giant, to health care equipment and aircraft servicing, jobs are leaving the U.S. for Mexico, and NAFTA is encouraging this flight. (AFL-CIO Task Force on Trade 1993:31)

While expressing such apprehension whenever they had the chance, the unions were also careful to link NAFTA to union members' job security. For instance, when they appealed for support from unionized public employees who might think themselves unaffected by NAFTA, union officers argued that there would be job losses and plant closings in the wake of NAFTA, soon followed by budget cuts by states and localities, and then pressure for job cuts and lower wages for public workers. In short, uncontrolled foreign trade meant massive job displacement; not even government employees would be immune to its repercussions. The unions also drew comparisons between private sector employers' reasons for supporting NAFTA and public employers' attempts to downsize the workforce and contract out union work. They appealed for solidarity among workers facing comparable threats to their livelihood.

The unions turned NAFTA into a symbol of corporate power, greed, and arrogance—powerful terms at any time, but particularly so during the recession of the early 1990s, with its massive layoffs and plant closings. NAFTA, the unions contended, was meant to turn Mexico not into a huge market for American-made goods but rather into a low-wage production location for American factories (Donahue 1993a, b). Union members, having had firsthand experience with the power of corporations at the bargaining table and during organizing, were now being told that

NAFTA was just more of the same but at the international level. All workers, not just unionized workers, would be hurt: "We [the AFL-CIO] believe that [NAFTA] will serve to further weaken the U.S. manufacturing base, causing immeasurable pain and suffering to American workers" (AFL-CIO Task Force on Trade 1993:19). Jobs would be lost from "communities all across America" (AFL-CIO Task Force on Trade 1993:25). The unions claimed that half a million jobs, perhaps even a million, would be lost during the 1990s in the wake of NAFTA (Labor Advisory Committee 1992; AFL-CIO Task Force on Trade 1993).

The Executive Council of the AFL-CIO issued a statement calling on the Clinton administration to renegotiate rather than sign NAFTA: "To advance the public interest . . . a renegotiated NAFTA should stand up for worker rights, strong labor standards, consumer health and safety, and environmental protection" (AFL-CIO Executive Council 1993:1).

3. *NAFTA perpetuates unjust and unsuccessful economic policies.* The unions also linked NAFTA to economic policies that had led to economic dislocation and job losses since the early 1980s. For example, the Labor Advisory Committee (LAC), a labor group advising the government on foreign trade, made the connection between past, present, and future:

Under current trade arrangements, tens of thousands of U.S. workers have lost their jobs. Tens of thousands more have seen employment opportunities vanish as U.S. companies moved production to Mexico, taking advantage of the poverty of Mexican workers and the absence of any effective regulations on corporate behavior. The proposed free trade agreement will only make matters worse. (Labor Advisory Committee 1992:i)

NAFTA was also described as the product of a discredited economic theory:

Unfortunately, the NAFTA is simply the most recent manifestation of "trickle-down" economic theories—a rigidly ideological belief that overall progress eventually will be achieved if the organization and structure of economic and social affairs is left entirely to private capital. During the 1980 Republican presidential primaries, President Bush derided this simplistic ideology as "voodoo economics" with gains achieved through "smoke and mirrors." Now his administration proposes to compound the economic damage caused by this approach during the past 12 years by extending it to free trade with Mexico. (Labor Advisory Committee 1992:3).

In his congressional testimony, Thomas R. Donahue, AFL-CIO secretary-treasurer and the leading union spokesperson against NAFTA, made the same point: "NAFTA represents the most recent manifestation of trickle-down economics, coupled with reliance on the free market, as the only path to economic progress. It has not worked over the last 12 years, and it will not work now" (Donahue 1993a:44).

4. *NAFTA hurts rather than helps Mexican workers.* The unions showed concern rather than disdain for Mexican workers and Mexican society. This distinguished the unions from other NAFTA opponents such as Ross Perot, who repeatedly assailed Mexico as a corrupt and undemocratic nation intent on taking Americans' jobs (Golden 1993). The unions argued that NAFTA's benefits to the Mexican economy would not be felt by Mexican workers and their families.

During the presidential campaign of 1992, Bill Clinton, trying to stake out a position on NAFTA that would bridge those of supporters and opponents, supported NAFTA on the condition that it be accompanied by labor and environmental side agreements. Clinton negotiated an environmental side agreement which enabled him to hold on to a large share of the environmental movement (Behr

1993a). But the labor side agreement did not satisfy the unions.[3] This agreement, the North American Agreement on Labor Cooperation, created the Commission for Labor Cooperation to promote eleven labor principles: (1) freedom of association and protection of the right to organize, (2) the right to bargain collectively, (3) the right to strike, (4) prohibition of forced labor, (5) labor protection for children and young persons, (6) minimum employment standards, (7) elimination of employment discrimination, (8) equal pay for men and women, (9) prevention of occupational injuries and illnesses, (10) compensation in case of occupational injuries and illnesses, and (11) protection of migrant workers (Verma et al. 1996; Smith 1997). The Commission, however, has no remedial powers, and its terms of reference were worded in such a way that countries could opt out of actions by claiming important economic, social, cultural, and legislative differences (Burgoon 1995; Verma et al. 1996; Adams and Singh 1997).

The labor side agreement enabled the Clinton administration to claim that it had repaired NAFTA's shortcomings and gave political cover to members of Congress trying to justify their support of the pact (Cowie 1997; Hecker 1997). The unions argued that the agreement did not go far enough, that it was ineffective—trade sanctions could be applied only in the most extreme cases—and would weaken existing trade laws, and that it failed to protect fundamental rights to organize and bargain collectively (Adams and Singh 1997; Stevenson 1997).

The unions' rejection of the side agreement was phrased in a positive way and coupled with a broader concern for Mexicans. Mexicans, the unions proclaimed, must be helped to overcome their poverty, low wages, and harsh working conditions, but this should be done in a strong economy and a protected environment. Foreign aid and debt relief, rather than a trade pact with a weak side agreement, would lead to a better life for Mexicans (Davis 1992; AFL-CIO Executive Council 1993; AFL-CIO Task Force on Trade 1993).

"Mexican workers have no protection with which to ensure that they, not just their employers, benefit from increased investment so they might become consumers for the products that they and we produce," charged the Labor Advisory Committee (1992:i). Moreover, the AFL-CIO Task Force on Trade argued that there is "little likelihood that the Mexican masses will be able to buy many goods made in the United States . . . because their wages . . . do not translate into a standard of living comparable to that enjoyed by [Americans]" (1993:20). American companies would "increase profits on the backs of impoverished Mexican workers" (AFL-CIO Task Force on Trade 1993:25). A social activist with experience at Mexican plants was quoted as saying, "If NAFTA passes, Mexicans will be eating beans and rice, Americans will be flipping burgers and a few folks on Wall Street will be trading on our sweat and blood" (AFL-CIO Task Force on Trade 1993:41).

5. *You can oppose NAFTA and still support greater international trade.* Finally, the unions wanted to appear flexible in their approach to foreign trade. The case against NAFTA could not seem to be overtly protectionist—most right-wing opponents were taking this approach—but rather had to be presented as a considered response to the particulars of the agreement. To do this, the unions continually emphasized that the United States *should* engage in international trade and that close trading relationships between nations can result in economic growth. Their concern was with who would benefit from the increased trade under NAFTA,

> the small number on the top rungs of the economic ladder who did so well under the Reagan and Bush Administrations, or the vast numbers of workers on the bottom and middle rungs who have been left behind. . . . The AFL-CIO believes that it is time to try something different—an integrated economic, social and trade policy which promotes a high skill, high wage future for all Americans, not just the privileged few. (AFL-CIO 1992:1)

In short, NAFTA, not all foreign trade, was wrong. NAFTA had been drafted to provide investment opportunities for corporations rather than opportunities for economic and social betterment, the goals shared by the unions and their coalition partners. In a newspaper advertisement, the AFL-CIO declared, "When NAFTA is defeated, we will work together to write a new, fair trade agreement— an agreement that helps people throughout the hemisphere instead of exploiting them" ("NAFTA: Who Wins, Who Loses?" 1993:A20).

Despite the unions' efforts, NAFTA was passed. The House of Representatives voted 234 for and 200 against—not as close as most had predicted. The Senate, where passage was never seriously in doubt, approved NAFTA by a vote of 61 to 38 (Garland 1993). NAFTA went into effect in January 1994, creating the largest free trade area in the world, with a population of more than 360 million and a gross domestic product of more than $6 trillion (U.S. General Accounting Office 1993a). The labor side agreement that was so sharply criticized by the unions came into effect with NAFTA.

Although the unions were not powerful enough to blunt the offensive of the NAFTA supporters, particularly the Clinton administration, they were by no means powerless. By broadening the bases of their opposition, the unions and their partners shaped public opinion, though not far enough. In March 1991, 72 percent of Americans believed that the impact of NAFTA would be "mostly good" for the United States, and only 15 percent believed it would be "mostly bad." By September 1992, 55 percent said that NAFTA would be "mostly good" and 24 percent were against it. Only half the respondents had read or heard anything about NAFTA. Public awareness rose to 72 percent by a September 1993 survey. By then, only 35 percent of respondents supported NAFTA while 41 percent opposed it. Moreover, three times as many strongly opposed it (21 percent) as strongly favored it (7 percent). These figures remained fairly stable up to the House vote in November 1993, when 38 percent supported NAFTA and 41 percent opposed it (Robinson 1994; Burgoon 1995).

Robinson (1994:682–683) concluded that "President Clinton ultimately won his NAFTA fight in Congress not because most Americans were persuaded that the deal was a good one, but because they were evenly divided enough on the issue to give pro-NAFTA Republicans and Democrats the 'wiggle room' to support the deal without paying a high political price."[4]

Despite the outcome, the NAFTA campaign provided unions with an opportunity to gain moral legitimacy without relinquishing their pragmatic legitimacy among members. They were doing the right thing in the eyes of coalition partners and many among the general public because of their emphasis on issues that addressed broad concerns: the environment, the fundamental economic and social well-being of all Americans, general economic policies, the protection of Mexican workers, and international trade. At the same time, the unions showed their members that working through a coalition to fight legislation was directly related to their job security; the anti-NAFTA campaign was always seen by members as having pragmatic legitimacy and being tied to traditional union objectives in representation (protecting jobs and income from competition).

The campaign energized the unions. They framed the issues in such a way as to attract extensive participation from members who were often indifferent to their leaders' causes. They worked with coalition partners on the community as well as the national level, finding common ground in their apprehension over unrestrained trade. A regional leader of the coalition commented: "Trade is connected with everything. I go to a meeting where Teamsters sit down with Greenpeace and Catholic priests. It's the greatest coalition building issue I've ever seen" (Davis 1992:A1). In Portland, Oregon, for example, the coalition brought together timber workers and environmentalists, two groups that were often bitter foes (Behr 1993b).

In the previous chapter we saw how unions failed at their attempt to extend their domain of legitimate activities to include the provision of group benefits through associate membership. In contrast, with their NAFTA campaign the unions were able to recast their role as leaders in trade issues. They articulated a new vision of the global economy in which trade raises the condition of workers to humane levels across nations, an approach quite different from the extremes of promoting unlimited free trade or rejecting the expansion of trade on principle. Although the unions had called attention to global labor standards earlier, "it was only during the battle over NAFTA . . . that labor's fair trade strategy fully bloomed" (Burgoon 1995:11).

Working with their coalition, the unions blocked the president's attempt in November 1997 to use fast track negotiation for extending NAFTA to Chile and other Latin American nations (the first time a president had been denied fast track authority). With the slogan "NAFTA—Never Again!" they insisted that any new trade agreements would have to include strong provisions on labor and environmental issues rather than dealing with them through side agreements (Stevenson 1997).[5] This contention was evident again in December 1999 as the unions worked with a diverse coalition and were able to upset the meetings of the World Trade Organization in Seattle. They insisted that any new trade pacts must include, and not just be accompanied by, agreements on labor issues, and that these must impose sanctions against countries that violate basic labor standards and fail to protect workers' rights to organize (Greenhouse 1999c; Greenhouse and Kahn 1999). The unions claimed again that they were not merely protecting their members' jobs but engaging in a "comprehensive campaign for a fair society, [both] globally and nationally" (Moberg 2000:12).[6] Finally, in October 2000 a landmark trade agreement was signed between the United States and Jordan which required compliance with international labor and environmental standards (for example, multinational companies investing in Jordan must recognize workers' rights to join unions). These requirements were included in the text of the trade pact, not in side agreements. The AFL-CIO was active in drafting the pact's labor standards section, hailed by the Clinton administration as a new model for trade agreements (Kahn 2000b).

In summary, the unions' greatest gain in the campaign against NAFTA can best be understood in terms of their management of legitimacy. It was always clear throughout the campaign that unions were primarily concerned about job losses—an issue of critical importance to their members but less important to other coalition partners. But they demonstrated to their coalition partners, their members, and the public in general that their concerns appropriately extended well beyond collective bargaining gains (Edsall 1993). The fact that unions joined a common front in opposition to NAFTA—including even those, such as environmental groups, with whom unions were often at odds—lent strength and credence to their positions. The unions may have failed to block the trade pact, but they did succeed in showing that they could conform to the values of a wide range of constituencies.

The Massachusetts Nurses Association

Our final case describes a campaign organized by the Massachusetts Nurses Association (MNA) called the Statewide Campaign for Safe Care. It arose out of nurses' concerns that the quality of patient care was being harmed because mandatory overtime and cost-cutting efforts were reducing the employment of nurses and increasing the numbers of unlicensed personnel.[7]

The Statewide Campaign for Safe Care sought to introduce legislation and regulation to ensure patient access to safe nursing care. From the start of the campaign, the MNA presented a clear and consistent message: nurses are very much concerned about the quality of care that patients receive and want to make sure that patients get safe care; patient care is compromised, however, when there are not enough registered nurses on duty to provide direct clinical care. In a manner reminiscent of unions' efforts against NAFTA, the MNA managed legitimacy by identifying itself and its objectives with widely shared values and norms concerning patients' rights.

Nurses in Unions

Nurses first established a professional nursing association in 1896, when they founded the Nurses Associated Alumnae (later to become the American Nurses Association). The reasons for forming and joining a nurses' association were many:

> What finally drove nurses to unite? The proliferation of hospital schools of nursing, lack of standardization among the schools, lack of entrance standards, exploitation of nursing students as cheap sources of labor, and deplorable working conditions, including 11-hour workdays for hospital nurses and 24-hour shifts for private duty nurses for weeks at a time. There was also a desire by nurses to have a professional organization that would establish a code of ethics, elevate standards of nursing, and promote the interests of nurses. (Ketter 1996:1)

The Massachusetts Nurses Association was founded in 1903 as a chapter of the American Nurses Association and the largest association of health care workers in the state. Mary Manning, the MNA's executive director, in an interview with the authors identified the driving forces behind its formation as essentially the same as the ones that exist today: a desire to protect the patient and the profession.

In 1946 the American Nurses Association (ANA) unanimously adopted an economic security program that included collective bargaining. That same year the MNA adopted its own bargaining program, but the Massachusetts Supreme Court ruled that hospitals, as charitable institutions, were not covered by collective bargaining laws. It was not until 1965 that the MNA successfully lobbied for legislation extending bargaining protection to RNs and other hospital employees. Two years later it held its first representation election, won bargaining rights, and negotiated its first contract (Flanagan 1983; Ketter 1996).

Until 1968 the ANA maintained a no-strike policy. Because it was also illegal for nurses to strike in some states, nurses engaged instead in mass resignations to affect bargaining outcomes. Recognizing its inability to control this policy—mass resignations could be defined by courts as strikes—and expressing a desire "to maintain high standards of patient care in hospitals" (Ketter 1996:21), the ANA rescinded the no-strike policy, and state associations were left to determine their own policies. Still, few strikes occurred because the National Labor Relations Act did not extend protection to employees of private, not-for-profit hospitals. Strikers could be replaced and bargaining rights jeopardized.[8] Coverage was extended, however, under the Health Care Amendments of 1974, and this led to an increase in the number of health care workers covered by contracts, though not the number of strikes (Ketter 1996).[9]

The extension of collective bargaining laws to private nonprofit hospitals had two major effects. First, it encouraged traditional labor unions, not just professional associations, to organize the sector. Management began to scrutinize its personnel policies to identify and deal with sources of discontent in anticipation of possible organizing and bargaining. Second, there was a new receptiveness among nurses to collective bargaining and a belief that it was compatible with professionalism (evident at that time also in the expanding union representation of teachers and social workers). Organizers argued that collective bargaining could emphasize professional responsibilities to ensure quality care by protecting nurses' autonomy in the health care setting and giving them a voice in compensation decisions (Flanagan 1983; Goodman-Draper 1995).

Within a few years of the 1974 amendments, there was a spurt in the organization of nurses by unions of professional and service workers as well as chapters of the ANA. Organizing contests in hospitals increased threefold from 1974 to 1977, and union density in hospitals rose slightly from 13 percent in 1974 to 17 percent in 1981, then fluctuated between 15 and 18 percent over the next fifteen years (Hirsch and Schumacher 1998). A key barrier to further unionization was the paternalism common to hospitals; the nurse's role was still seen predominantly as that of an obedient "giver of service," and health care employers were expected to "bestow the proper benefits at the proper time" (Flanagan 1983:16). Unions and professional associations countered by arguing that if nurses did not engage in collective bargaining over compensation, decisions on staffing and working conditions would be made by management, with less concern for quality care.

In recent years, federal reimbursement has changed dramatically, putting pressure on hospitals to cut costs. Nurses now face intense pressure and loss of control: "Downsizing, Work Restructuring, Mergers, Acquisitions, Cost Control, Layoffs, Managed Care Networks. These words signal dramatic changes in the health care system—changes that in too many cases are having a negative impact on the nursing profession and the quality of patient care" (Massachusetts Nurses Association 1995a:5).

The main force behind the spread of unionization has been the nurses' belief that management was "de-skilling" their jobs, that is, attempting to reduce costs by having components of the nurse's job performed by less skilled workers (Greene 1998). A 1991 survey for ANA found that two-thirds of responding nurses would support an organizing drive for collective bargaining.[10] Unionized nurses receive higher pay than nonunion ones (by about 8 percent), although this may reflect the fact that they are primarily employed on the East and West coasts and at larger, higher-paying institutions. Union and nonunion nurses generally enjoy similar employment benefits (pensions and health care plans). ANA leaders emphasize, however, that the de-skilling of nurses' jobs and patient care problems such as short staffing have been more important in leading nurses to unionize than inadequate wages and benefits (Lippman

1991). Nurses complained that their concerns were not being heeded and that patient care was at risk. This feeling is captured, for example, by the comments of an emergency room nurse who voted for union representation during a 1999 organizing drive in Cleveland: "We have voiced our opinions in the past. But I don't think we were ever heard. Now that we have formed a union we'll have a voice in the decisions that affect our patients and our profession at a time when we never needed it more" (Gonzalez 1999:2b).

The stated mission of the MNA is "to be a unified voice and the professional home of registered nurses, committed to advancing the highest quality health care in a continually changing environment" (Massachusetts Nurses Association 1998a:1). The MNA's primary activities are collective bargaining, lobbying, and education. Its institutional goal is to be seen as the professional association of nurses, with a role akin to that of the state Bar Association (although it must be noted that Massachusetts has not, nor has any other state, established membership in a nurses association as a requirement to practice).

In 1998 there were over 120,000 nurses in Massachusetts, of whom 19,000 were members of the MNA. Eighty-five percent of the members were covered by collective bargaining agreements (Goldstein 1998).[11] In 1997 the MNA negotiated 36 collective agreements, pursued over 1,000 grievances, filed 15 unfair labor practice charges with labor relations boards, and represented nurses at 79 arbitration hearings over grievances (Massachusetts Nurses Association 1998b).

Not all MNA members are employed nurses. The association actively recruits graduating student nurses as full members, making a strong effort to promote itself at nursing schools. Although the MNA does not represent these nurses in dealings with employers, they are nonetheless full members.

The MNA's bylaws include a clause that insulates those members covered by collective agreements from those who are supervisory nurses. Only members in collective bargaining units can serve on the Cabinet for Labor Relations (the MNA's governing structure for determining bargaining policy). Without such separation, members and other unions could claim that the MNA is not qualified to serve as a bargaining agent because managers exercise control over it. Each bargaining unit of the MNA is nearly autonomous, with its officers permitted to write bylaws and administer the chapter. The MNA's Labor Relations Department provides resources and expertise to the local bargaining units, and the MNA exercises final approval over all contracts.

Many of the services offered by the MNA reflect its professional orientation. For example, its Career Center offers counseling, workshops, a résumé critique service, and networking sessions for new graduates as well as nurses forced or choosing to leave a position. Its Massachusetts Nurses Foundation offers scholarships and grants and supports research and the publication of research on nursing topics (Massachusetts Nurses Association 1998).

The Statewide Campaign for Safe Care

In the early 1990s, the MNA's officers were hearing with increased frequency from nurses concerned about working conditions and patient safety. This was at a time of hospital restructuring through mergers, the elimination of departments and the downsizing of hospital staff, and the rising use of unlicensed assistive personnel and mandatory overtime. Believing that the issue reflected important industrywide trends and not isolated incidents, the MNA chose to respond on a statewide basis. In August 1994 the MNA announced a public campaign for quality care. Margaret Barry, president of the MNA, framed the issue as one of patient safety:

> The safety of our patients has always been the tie that binds all nurses together. It only seems right for this association to make patient safety, and nursing's role as the guarantor of that safety the common ground upon which we will make an aggressive

stand in the media, the professional community, the legislature and the workplace. (Massachusetts Nurses Association 1994a:1)

The MNA began a series of town meetings for RNs practicing in hospitals (town meetings were also held for nurses in community health). The first meeting, in September 1994, drew about 220 nurses:

The purpose of the meeting . . . was to solicit input from members about the issue of patient safety and how we might address this issue. Specifically, those attending were asked to consider and speak to the following three questions: Is there a patient safety problem; how do you define patient safety; and what are the factors contributing to the lack of patient safety? (Massachusetts Nurses Association 1994a:2)

About fifty nurses spoke out, identifying problems related to systemic changes such as cost cutting and the growth of managed care. There was broad consensus about the problems but less agreement about how to proceed. Some nurses felt that by making these problems known, they might scare patients and jeopardize the institutions they worked for. The overwhelming sentiment, however, was that statewide action was needed. The idea for a Statewide Campaign for Safe Care grew out of this meeting.

Over the next eighteen months, town meetings were held throughout Massachusetts, primarily to form Local Action Committees (LACs) for developing and implementing safe care activities at the local levels, and for building visibility and support for nurses. Using the theme "Every Patient Deserves a Nurse," the LACs emphasized the positive link between RN care and patient outcomes and promoted the MNA's legislative agenda. To aid in this effort, the MNA distributed a large number of wallet-sized cards stating the campaign's theme and related information as a way to persuade the public that "the quality of care they receive in the heath care system is dependent upon their access to adequate levels of nursing care" (Massachusetts Nurses Association 1995b:12).

The MNA also brought representatives from other organizations into the Safe Care Campaign. In October 1995 it held a town meeting for other nursing groups: over seventy nursing leaders attended, representing twenty-two nursing organizations and schools. With the exception of the Massachusetts Organization of Nursing Executives—the association of nurses in administrative positions—the groups endorsed the campaign. In November of the same year, the MNA held a town meeting for key consumer advocacy organizations in the state. The MNA's leader, Margaret Barry, stated:

> Because of the controversial and complex nature of this issue, this is not a campaign that can be waged by nurses alone. Success can only be achieved through broad based participation and involvement by a powerful coalition of providers and consumers working together to make safe, quality care a reality. (quoted in Massachusetts Nurses Association 1995c:3)

Among the groups represented at the town meeting were the American Association of Retired People, the American Cancer Society, Headstart, the Massachusetts Medical Society, the Massachusetts Women's Health Care Coalition, and Boston Health Care for the Homeless. In a manner similar to earlier town meetings of nurses, this meeting concluded with breakout groups which gave participants an opportunity to share concerns. Discussions revealed that the "vast majority of those constituencies represented at the meeting had, in fact, seen the quality of care their members receive deteriorate in recent years" (Massachusetts Nurses Association 1996a:3).

The Legislative Agenda

The leaders of the MNA felt strongly that to maintain momentum, the campaign had to go beyond identifying problems and develop solutions. This was done through educational efforts and the promotion of a legislative agenda. During the first year of the Statewide Campaign for Safe Care, the MNA put together an expert group of practicing nurses, nurse managers, and teachers and asked them to write legislation addressing the problems identified at the town meetings. The group's work formed the basis of a legislative packet, The Nurses' Agenda for Quality Care, which included model laws requiring identification of health care providers and levels of nursing care. The MNA stressed the importance of this requirement:

> Patients have the right to know who is caring for them. Studies and interviews have revealed that it is often difficult for the public to identify a physician from a nurse, or from an unlicensed aide.... This legislation simply mandates that the patient should see an identifying label of licensure status on the person who is caring for them.... The pin will identify your "RN" licensure status. It therefore prohibits the homogenization of the provider to the status of "multi-skilled worker" or "patient care associate," which is a common tactic of hospital reengineering schemes. (Massachusetts Nurses Association 1996b:1)

This legislation was signed into law in December 1996 and required all persons who deliver health care to patients to wear appropriate identification.

The legislative packet also included An Act to Ensure Sufficient Nursing Care, model legislation that would require institutions to provide adequate nursing care. It would create a formula and provide specific language for determining sufficient levels of care. It also included "whistle-blower" protection for employees reporting unsafe levels of nursing care or unsafe conditions caused by staffing changes (Goldstein 1998; Mann 1998).

The proposed legislation faced stiff opposition from the Massachusetts Organization of Nurse Executives and hospital officials who felt that mandatory minimums for nursing staff would be unworkable given the rapid changes in the number of patients and severity of illness. One state representative said that the legislature was "hesitant to impose regulations such as minimum nursing staff given the fast paced change in the health care industry" (Precht 1997:35). The bill died in committee, but the legislature did include a provision in the state budget for the creation of the Special Commission on the Delivery of Health Care Services by Nurses. This commission was given the task of investigating the impact of regulations and policies on the delivery of nursing care, including the safety implications of staffing levels. The MNA considered this a partial victory; though not the legislation the association had sought, it was a first step for a bipartisan investigation that could lead to guarantees of safe staffing levels (Massachusetts Nurses Association 1999b).

The MNA filed separate whistle-blower legislation. The issue received a great deal of publicity in early 1998, much of it centered on a nurse who was fired for reporting unsafe patient care conditions (a federal judge ruled that the nurse had been illegally fired). After hearings in which no one testified against it, the bill was approved by the state Senate. Similar legislation was passed by the Massachusetts House (Bureau of National Affairs 1999), and funds for the enforcement of whistle-blower protection were included in the state's budget for the 2000 fiscal year (Massachusetts Nurses Association 1999a, b).

UAPs and Contract Negotiations

The Statewide Campaign for Safe Care initially grew out of nurses' concerns about the effects of cost cutting, one of the most troubling aspects of which was the use of unlicensed assistive personnel (UAP). UAPs are entrusted with such tasks as inserting and removing catheters, taking vital signs, and drawing blood samples. In most states, including Massachusetts, UAPs do not have to meet minimum educational or training levels or pass an exam, and unlike aides in nursing homes, they do not need to meet federally mandated standards.[12]

Supporters of the use of UAPs, among them the state hospital associations, say that they free nurses to do what nurses are trained to do. They also argue that nurses are concerned about UAPs only because their job security is being threatened. Because of the increased emphasis on outpatient care and the decreasing number of hospital beds, hospitals must adjust to a declining market. This cannot be accomplished by keeping on staff a large number of RNs who are highly paid relative to UAPs (Kunen 1996).

But others, including nurses' associations, claim that the use of UAPs is dictated only by cost savings and puts patients at risk. Cases of incompetence are cited. For example, a child in Rhode Island died when an aide put potassium chloride into her intravenous line instead of saline solution; a hospital in Ohio was successfully sued for its cost-cutting measures when a woman died because nurses' aides were not trained to notice early signs of infection; a man in Pennsylvania died when an aide mistakenly hooked up a feeding tube to the opening in his neck that helped him breathe; and an aide in Boston kept feeding an elderly burn patient, who subsequently died, failing to notice that she was not swallowing the food.

Supporters of the use of UAPs dismiss such evidence as purely anecdotal, claiming that nursing leaders, particularly those in the associations that act as bargaining agents, are merely trying to save nurses' jobs even if doing so perpetuates less than efficient operations (Twedt 1996a). But their opponents point to thousands of such stories as well as to the research of Judith Shindul-Rothschild which suggests that hospitals endanger patients when they use more UAPs. Her detractors, many of them hospital administrators, believe her research to be biased because she interviews only nurses. But she has publicly responded by challenging hospitals to provide data showing that the quality of care has not declined with the increased use of UAPs (Twedt 1996b).[13]

The use of UAPs has become an important aspect of nurses' contract negotiations in Massachusetts. Although no strikes have actually occurred, strike votes have been called in which the use of UAPs was an issue. For example, at Brigham and Women's Hospital in Boston, it was a central issue for nurses in the September 1996 strike vote. According to a newspaper report:

> Both sides have battled bitterly for more than a year over a new contract. While administrators say the issues mainly revolve around pay and work conditions, nurses insist they are fighting to protect patient care by preventing unlicensed aides from performing some duties that have traditionally been the province of registered nurses. (Lewis and Pham 1996:A4)

A final agreement, reached without a strike, included a clause stating that the assignment of any job or duty to a UAP would be done at the sole discretion of a registered nurse.

The agreement negotiated with Cape Cod Hospital went the furthest in incorporating safe care language in general, and on UAPs in particular. Fixed staffing levels for every floor and every department were established, and nurses gained the right to refuse to delegate duties to UAPs (Massachusetts Nurses Association 1997).

But the MNA was not always successful in getting the desired provisions into contracts. At the Berkshire Medical Center in Pittsfield, Massachusetts, a deadlock in negotiations occurred when management resisted nurses' demands for language that would allow them to refuse to delegate certain duties to UAPs. The union took a strike vote: 75 percent voted to strike, but the union bylaws required 85 percent. Management was strongly opposed to the nurses' demand, claiming that the Berkshire nurses were being used as a test case by the MNA to secure its model of safe patient care in the contract (Lahr 1997a). The nurses eventually ratified by a vote of 199 to 135 a two-year contract that did not include the desired language.

The Statewide Campaign for Safe Care has not only figured prominently in contract negotiations but also improved the MNA's visibility and credibility among nurses. One newspaper article referred to a "speed-up" at the MNA. "A few years ago, the association got one call a month from nurses trying to organize unions. Now the calls come in daily" ("Health Care Squeeze" 1998:1). MNA spokespersons see synergies between bargaining (which has received widespread publicity) and organizing; unorganized nurses believe they have the same problems as organized ones, but without a representative they believe matters can only get worse. According to one organizer, a surgical floor nurse at a hospital where nurses voted for the union in early 1998, " 'Patient safety, patient care and the [desire] to practice nursing the way we learned to do it' propelled the nurses to get a bargaining agent" (quoted in Hammel 1998).[14]

The Public Portrayal

Newspaper coverage has been favorable to the MNA's concerns. Articles usually begin with anecdotes about patients who have been harmed or died, accompanied by quotations from MNA representatives. For example:

When Rosalie Zucco went to Good Samaritan Medical Center for major cancer surgery on a lung, she took comfort in thinking nurses would be with her every step of the way. But when the 59-year-old Holbrook woman came out of intensive care and was placed in a room, she quickly found that nurses were hard to find. . . . The Massachusetts Nurses Association says Zucco's case is a symptom of potentially unsafe staffing levels at some hospitals, which are cutting costs by slowly replacing nurses with lesser-trained and lower-paid aides ("The Changing Role of Nurses" 1997:1).

Statewide trends are described to suggest the seriousness of the problem:

In hospitals across Massachusetts, experienced nurses are being replaced by unlicensed aides who receive only minimal training before being allowed to care for patients. Doctors and nurses say the practice is dangerous and fear what will happen to hospital care as unlicensed aides take over more duties (Lasalandra 1997:1).

Coverage of contract negotiations and strike votes consistently portray nurses as concerned about patient care. In the case of the Berkshire Medical Center, nurses were described in the local paper as engaged in an "ongoing fight for a job contract they believe will ensure patient safety" (Lahr 1997b:A1) and unwilling to budge on five key matters, "all of which relate in one way or another to what the nurses refer to as 'safe patient care' and what management refers to as 'job security'" (Lahr 1997:A1).

The MNA as Patient Advocate

The MNA never denied that it wanted to protect jobs; indeed, the protection of nursing jobs was clearly at the heart of the campaign. For example, establishing safe levels of care was predicated on the employment of registered nurses. Limiting the number of UAPs meant higher staffing levels of RNs. Attempts to abolish mandatory overtime reflected a desire to ensure adequate numbers of nurses and to protect nurses from long hours of work. Detractors sought to present the MNA as an interest group attempting to preserve members' jobs at whatever cost necessary. But their claims that the MNA was trying to block needed efficiencies was not nearly as compelling to the public or as widely accepted in the media as the MNA's claim that patient care was being compromised by management's pursuit of efficiency.

When we examine the campaign from a legitimacy perspective, we see the association's members, coalition partners, and the public conferring moral legitimacy on the MNA: protecting patients is unambiguously good. With its central and compatible values of preserving patient care and protecting nurses' jobs, the campaign managed legitimacy as it appealed to its different constituencies. For members, it certainly met instrumental ends and enhanced pragmatic legitimacy, while it also cast nurses as a crucial and endangered component of quality health care. For coalition partners—which included a wide range of advocacy groups representing, among others, the elderly and children—the campaign addressed their primary considerations, that is, the safety of their constituencies. The public, though concerned about rising costs when they viewed the health care industry as a whole, were likely to be more concerned about the quality of services than with the efficiency and cost effectiveness with which the services are provided. And the MNA's concern with both patient care and job protection increased its appeal to any unorganized nurses who may have had second thoughts about whether unionization was compatible with professional values.

The MNA became associated with widely shared norms concerning the quality of care that patients deserve. The Statewide Campaign for Safe Care consistently emphasized quality. All of the publicity material, spokespersons, and members spoke with a unified voice: hospitalized patients have a right to quality care, and RNs are essential to providing that care. The media coverage accepted that nurses are concerned with patient safety and attributed problems to the lack of RNs. Through its management of moral legitimacy, the MNA was able to show how each of its traditional activities—organizing, bargaining, and political action—was a crucial component in the campaign, not merely the unrelated activities of a narrowly based interest group.

NAFTA and MNA: Unifying Themes

The two cases presented in this chapter are similar in three respects. First, in both cases the unions managed legitimacy by identifying existing processes and goals with widely shared values and norms. Both the campaign against NAFTA and the Safe Care campaign were engaged in a traditional union activity, lobbying, with the explicit goal of protecting jobs—against the forces of unrestricted foreign trade in one case and the use of lesser-skilled workers in the other case. Both groups (the entire union movement in one case, the MNA in the other) presented themselves as confronting a threat that extended well beyond the job concerns of members. They demonstrated that what they did and why they did it were fully compatible with widely shared values and norms, as expressed by the five themes promoted by the unions in the anti-NAFTA campaign and by the concern for patient safety in the statewide campaign of the nurses.

Second, in both cases the unions were appealing to essentially the same constituencies—the general public, coalition partners, and members. And third, the unions gained moral as well as pragmatic legitimacy from their coalition partners and the public. Although the MNA had not had contentious relationships with its many and diverse coalition partners (these ranged from medical societies to patient groups), as had the unions fighting NAFTA, the bases for the coalitions were nevertheless the same: the proposed legislation affected their common interests. For example, the MNA's coalition partners representing patient groups feared a deterioration of patient care for their constituents. The anti-NAFTA coalition partners sought environmental or human rights protections.

In chapter 2 we saw that legitimacy can be especially problematic for organizations with diverse constituencies. In the NAFTA example in particular, some of the organizations with which the union was now collaborating had clashed with it in the past. Coalition activities may also create closer scrutiny by members if there is concern that the union is neglecting workplace representation (a basis for pragmatic legitimacy). This was not an issue for either the anti-NAFTA or nurses' campaign because protecting union members' jobs was a central (though not the only) theme. In the anti-NAFTA campaign, concern for jobs was reflected directly in two of the five themes: NAFTA would affect the fundamental social and economic well-being of all Americans (i.e., many jobs would be lost), and NAFTA would perpetuate unjust and unsuccessful economic policies (i.e., it would lead to severe economic dislocation and related job losses). The rights of Mexican workers were advocated, but not at the expense of American workers and union members.

With the MNA's Safe Care campaign, the union successfully linked together a broad concern for patient care with the protection of nursing jobs. Because health care costs are a central concern to so many Americans, detractors sought to equate the use of RNs with high costs and portrayed the RNs' efforts as simply trying to protect expensive jobs. So seamlessly had the MNA's themes been promoted, however, that its detractors' position received little or no support from the media and coalition partners representing patients. In both cases, NAFTA and the MNA, unions presented consistent themes with no ambiguity, successfully linking the protection of their members with issues of importance to other constituencies.

Though crucial themes for members, saving union jobs and strengthening unions were not unifying or motivating themes for the coalition partners. This distinction, while obvious, has important implications in the context of legitimacy. In both cases the public or coalition partners conferred legitimacy on unions as institutions but on particular actions. To return to the example at the beginning of chapter 2, banks as institutions have moral legitimacy, not just their activities. In each instance in this chapter, it was *what the unions did* that gained moral legitimacy, not *the unions themselves.* The public, that is, supported the need to protect workers' jobs that underlay the anti-NAFTA campaign or the right of patients to have licensed, highly trained RNs care for them when hospitalized. In these campaigns, the public conferred moral legitimacy on union efforts to "do the right thing." There is no indication, however, that this support diffuses to become moral legitimacy for the unions as organizations.

These cases present further evidence of why legitimacy creates problems for unions. As we see once again, maintaining pragmatic legitimacy by meeting members' instrumental demands may require a union simultaneously to seek moral legitimacy from other constituencies whose support is necessary. But if moral legitimacy does not extend beyond a particular event or campaign to encompass unions as an institution, the burden of proof is continually on unions to show that their traditional activities transcend parochial concerns. At the same time, unions must respond to pressure from their members to maintain pragmatic legitimacy.

CHAPTER 5

What Can Legitimacy Tell Us about the State of the Unions?

When we first started work on this book, we were quite pessimistic about the state of the unions. All signs pointed to low levels of legitimacy as well as a continuing decline in membership and influence. The dire predictions about the near disappearance of unions in the first decades of the new millennium did not seem far-fetched. The sole source of legitimacy appeared to be among unions' members and coalition partners, and then only when an issue united them. Nonmembers seemed uninterested, employers openly hostile, and public commitment to the continued existence of unions appeared to be virtually nonexistent. In sum, few were likely to be upset should unions disappear from our society and economy.

Our initial goal was to understand better the decline of unions, in the hope that a new perspective might suggest strategies that traditional approaches have overlooked. As a concept, legitimacy had great intuitive appeal. We found that the term appeared frequently in discussions of contemporary unions and was increasingly being used in industrial relations research. Although these references showed that its uses and definitions varied among authors, certain themes emerged. First, legitimacy is conferred by, and reflects the expectations of, different constituencies. Second, unions operate in strong institutional environments. Legitimacy is a central force in such environments because it affects an organization's access to valuable resources, whether monetary, political, or social.

As we began our case studies, our initial pessimism was rekindled. Drawing the crucial distinction between pragmatic, moral, and cognitive legitimacy presented a bleak picture of the state of unions. Cognitive legitimacy—that taken-for-granted quality—is nonexistent for unions. Moral legitimacy—being perceived as doing the right thing—is rare; it is conferred either on particular activities (such as the MNA's Safe Care Campaign) or on unions as institutions by only a few among their constituencies (for example, some coalition partners). The legitimacy conferred on unions, where it existed, was usually pragmatic, resting on the self-interested calculations of the unions' constituencies. They were asking: Do unions provide me with a benefit or service that is, on the whole, valuable? Do I gain more than I lose by being or becoming a union member, by being covered by a collective agreement, by working with a union in a coalition, by negotiating with a union, or by having a union represent me at my company?

The richness of the concept of legitimacy became increasingly evident. Legitimacy mattered to the unions in our case studies. Without it, for example, the Teamsters would not have won public support for a strike that inconvenienced countless numbers of businesses and individuals. With it, unions might have been able to extend their traditional activities to include associate membership with group benefits.

But legitimacy was also problematic. Unions could not assume that they had legitimacy as an institution. They had to generate legitimacy around issues: the safe care of patients, the unfairness of NAFTA, the rights of part-time workers. The task of shaping legitimacy is a difficult one for unions in an era when they are weakened by management opposition, membership decline, and competitive pressures from the expanding nonunion sector of the economy. Unions face the often daunting task of defending or regaining legitimacy as it is increasingly questioned by constituencies. Ashforth and Gibbs (1990) observed how such a situation creates a vicious circle: when an organization argues too loudly that it still has and deserves legitimacy, it may only cause constituencies to question whether this is so. When unions try overtly to generate legitimacy, this can cause constituencies to question whether they deserve it.

But analysis of the cases also provided hope for unions because it showed that unions can successfully manage and gain legitimacy in their traditional roles. Unions are not, and do not need to be, passive recipients of legitimacy. Unions can be active and skillful managers of legitimacy, as evidenced by the union organizing at Harvard, the MNA's Statewide Campaign for Safe Care, and the Teamsters' strike at UPS.

We have used the concept of legitimacy as a lens for analyzing unions in five different contexts: striking, organizing, offering a new form of membership, fighting proposed legislation, and promoting a statewide agenda. This lens focuses our attention on different forms of legitimacy, different strategies for managing legitimacy, and the role and importance of different constituencies. It leads us back to the two broad conclusions with which we began this book: that legitimacy matters and that it is problematic. We gain a richer understanding of why legitimacy matters and what problems unions face as they manage legitimacy when we analyze our five cases in terms of constituencies, strategies, and types of legitimacy.

First, as we have discussed throughout, the unions did not have cognitive or moral legitimacy as institutions. Pragmatic legitimacy was not sufficient to achieve their ends; the unions needed the support of constituencies that believed in the rightness of their actions or cause. Although the cases gave reason for optimism about unions' ability to gain moral legitimacy, this does not extend beyond a particular event or campaign. Unions may have been seen as doing the right thing by the general public in terms of their campaign against NAFTA, for example, but that support has not spread to unions in general as an institution that can serve as the voice of workers (as well as consumers, environmentally concerned persons, and so on) on all trade matters. Similarly, the Teamsters were able to present the UPS strike as the right thing to do, but it is not clear that the Teamsters (or even unions in general) gained moral legitimacy that transcended the event, or that they became the acknowledged and unifying champion of part-time and full-time workers' rights in their response to threatening employment policies.

Our cases suggest that the most unions can do is repeatedly seek moral legitimacy on a situational basis in the hope that the cumulative effect will lead to a broader and more sustainable base for unions individually or as institutions. In short, so long as moral legitimacy is conferred on isolated activities (a particular strike or organizing or lobbying campaign), it must be continually renewed.

Second, many of the unions we studied managed either to adapt organizational processes and goals to conform to those perceived as legitimate, or to identify their existing processes and goals with widely shared values and norms. Such strategies make sense in the context in which unions operate. These are times of shrinking employment in unionized firms because of expanding foreign and domestic nonunion competition, declining union bargaining power, the spread of employment benefits and protection under labor laws rather than through unionization, and intense employer resistance to unions during organizing and bargaining. The unions have limited options: they can neither expect most constituencies to want or value what they offer automatically and enthusiastically, nor can they change what constituencies want and value to correspond to what unions offer. Considered within the context of managing legitimacy, the Harvard campaign shows the union adapting its tactics to reflect the workers' need for both instrumental gains and a sense of doing the right thing through a community of workers. Unions became leaders in the NAFTA coalition by identifying their goals with those of other coalition members. The MNA sought to protect members' jobs by associating the loss of RNs' jobs with the health care concerns shared by a wide variety of groups. The UPS strike linked the protection of UPS workers' jobs with the plight of all part-time workers, the insecurities of all full-time workers, and the desire to fight back against greedy and uncaring employers.

Third, the cases also strongly suggest that most constituencies do not expect unions to deviate from their usual activities. This was reflected in the problems associated with introducing the group benefits program as well as in the MNA campaign and union members' support of the campaign against NAFTA and the UPS strike. Even the nontraditional organizing campaign at Harvard had the goal of gaining higher wages and benefits and stronger workplace protection, all to be achieved through collective bargaining after union certification. Members appreciated the economic gains provided by their union, not just the new sense of community at work.

When we consider the choice of strategy and the unions' continual need to reinforce moral legitimacy, however, we believe that unions cannot passively assume that constituencies will find what they do to be of general social value (that is, will confer moral legitimacy). Such an approach is essentially tradition-bound—using traditional tactics in the pursuit of traditional objectives, with the expectation that these will become or remain wanted and valued if only their arguments can be made clearly and forcefully.

All of this does not translate into full and lasting support for unions and their activities. In the absence of cognitive legitimacy, and with weak or absent moral legitimacy, there is no sense of the inviolability of unions. Many constituencies are indifferent as to whether unions continue to exist, and others (union members in particular) may care but for primarily instrumental reasons. For example, surveys show that union members are generally satisfied with unions, but there seems to be little depth to their feeling. Unions are commonly seen by members as their bargaining agents—service providers—for which they pay dues and receive benefits and protection. Significantly, the vast majority of members have never experienced their jobs on a nonunion basis or selected unionism during an organizing campaign. They went to work at a unionized enterprise and found that to be, on the whole, a satisfactory experience. Most joined unions under conditions in which nonmembership was not even perceived as an option. But the unions' inability to expand to any appreciable degree suggests the inadequacy of a strategy based primarily on an assumption that pragmatic legitimacy is sufficient to attract new members, to retain present ones, and to maintain an influential position in the economy.

In summary, the challenge for unions is to pursue moral and pragmatic legitimacy simultaneously because, as the cases suggest, neither can be pursued to the neglect of the other. Pragmatic legitimacy is crucial and forms the foundation of the unions' mission. Labor laws that certify union bargaining status as well as employers', workers', and the public's expectations are based on and reaffirm the importance of instrumentality. What unions do is not "right" in some abstract sense: unionization and representation in bargaining are not commonly seen as the inherent, inviolable civil right of workers. Rather, unions assume the practical role of agents that balance the power of employers at the workplace, that encode workers' rights in legally binding contracts, and that use the possibility of conflict to negotiate over a limited range of issues. Unions establish a government of the workplace that can be evaluated in terms of negotiated settlements and contract enforcement. In other words, the unions' constituencies, ranging from nonmembers to employers, have been conditioned by sixty years or more of labor relations practice to think in terms of conferring pragmatic legitimacy. As we have argued throughout, however, moral legitimacy is often critical for gaining the support necessary to achieve instrumental goals— the bases for pragmatic legitimacy.

We saw no evidence of cognitive legitimacy in our cases or in our review of the industrial relations literature, and we believe it is not possible at this time for unions to change this situation. Unions are not taken for granted and are not likely to be, at least in the near future. Even a fervent advocate of workers' rights could conceive of an America without unions; the unions as an institution would be gone, but workers could be protected by a greatly expanded body of labor laws and could participate in management decisions, including those involving wages and working conditions, by committees formed at workplaces and given enforceable powers by law. It would be difficult to conceive of our society without hospitals and public schools, or our economy without banks and privately held companies; we can hardly say the same for unions if alternative and effective forms of worker protection and representation were somehow devised.

Our intent is not to develop a sweeping explanation of why unions do what they do, why workers form and join them, or what the unions' role is, or should be, in our society. We do not propose a theory of the labor movement, or a general theory of union growth and decline. Rather, our contribution is the use of the concept of legitimacy as a lens for seeing unions anew. Legitimacy provides a frame of reference for understanding the sources of union strengths and weaknesses. It enables us to understand why some strategies, such as selectively broadening appeals in organizing drives, have been successful while others, such as providing consumer-oriented services to potential members, have not. And viewing unions in the context of legitimacy lets us see them both as organizations confined to certain avenues of activities by the widely shared expectations and values of constituencies and as organizations capable of managing legitimacy, that is, by changing the way they present themselves to conform to those expectations and values.

The focus on legitimacy also shows us, in a clear and vivid way, the bind that unions are in. Pragmatic legitimacy predominates, but it is weak. Moral legitimacy is rare and difficult to sustain, but it can go far toward strengthening (though not replacing) pragmatic legitimacy. Our society's entire way of thinking—from an employer's perspective when dealing with a union to a worker's consideration of voting for a union in an organizing drive—is set on a solid foundation of instrumentality. We have been conditioned to look for the value of the union in its ability to counter the power of the employer, not in its espousal of broad social objectives or promotion of justice in the workplace. Essentially, this pragmatic legitimacy places unions in the vulnerable position of being judged in terms of how well they promote the self-interests of those they represent. When the net gains seem unfavorable, nonunion workers reject organizing overtures and employers try to escape having to deal with unions. Most often there is no underlying ideology, just the pursuit of self-interest by different constituencies.

This is vividly illustrated in what was perhaps the unions' grandest attempt to date to gain moral legitimacy. The unions assumed a leadership role in the diverse coalition demonstrating at the meetings of the World Trade Organization in Seattle in 1999. They made a strong case, derived in large part from their earlier campaign against NAFTA, that those who promote global trade should also promote improved labor standards worldwide. Global trade should not incite a "race to the bottom" in which countries compete for industry and trade by offering the lowest wages and poorest working conditions. American unions portrayed themselves as fighting to protect the wages and job of workers internationally, not just in the United States. If this characterization was accepted by their constituencies, the unions would gain moral legitimacy for their actions and goals. But free trade proponents in the United States and among other member countries of the World Trade Organization sensed the weakness of American unions because of their heavy reliance on pragmatic legitimacy, even though the unions were working through a diverse coalition that included environmentalists and human rights groups. When the unions and their allies demanded that sanctions be imposed against nations that violate labor standards, this demand was attacked at home and abroad as blatant protectionism: the unions, critics charged, were conveniently finding a socially attractive way to ban imports that jeopardized their members' jobs rather than pursuing loftier goals of helping workers elsewhere (Greenhouse and Kahn 1999; Irwin 1999; Wysocki 1999; Sanger 1999a). Charges of promoting their own interests were again leveled against the unions in 2000 by the successful proponents of permanent normal trade relations with China (Greenhouse 2000a, b). Union opposition suffered from "the label of 'protectionism,'" of being "concerned about saving the jobs of union members at the expense of the American economy in general" (Clymer 2000:43).

Finally, the concept of legitimacy enables us to look afresh at the state of union movements in other countries. We can ask, for example, whether unions elsewhere enjoy pragmatic as well as moral legitimacy, or perhaps even cognitive legitimacy; whether one form of legitimacy can be managed by unions in ways that strengthen or lead to others; and whether these unions, facing declining membership and influence, have similar legitimacy concerns as those in the United States.

As an illustration, when we read of the declining influence of the once powerful German unions, we again recognize the vulnerability that comes with heavy reliance on pragmatic legitimacy and the failure to manage legitimacy carefully. Once the envy of unions everywhere because of their size and strength, German unions sought to ensure that the postwar prosperity would be shared by workers as well as managers. They successfully negotiated shorter work weeks, longer vacations, and higher pay. But more recently these gains have been blamed for high unemployment and low foreign investment in Germany. Moreover, unions have been unable to counter the spread of global competition and have fallen into disfavor with both workers and the government because of their ineffectiveness and the high labor costs they were imposing on the economy. They lost 3.5 million members in the 1990s. The German unions' vaunted power was based on pragmatic legitimacy, on their success in bargaining and spreading economic gains throughout the workforce, rather than on a deep-seated moral legitimacy based on their pursuit of socially valued goals or cognitive legitimacy in the sense of a belief that a democratic Germany—indeed, all free societies—must always have unions. Under such conditions, appraisal by constituencies can change quickly, and unions once praised for their effectiveness are now seen in the opposite light. Declining pragmatic legitimacy underlies the simple comment of an industrial worker in southern Germany who quit his union: "The union achieved a lot in the past, but I don't see what it can do for me now" (Rohwedder 1999:A1).

We have emphasized it earlier, but we feel we must say it again: legitimacy matters to unions. We urge those who formulate the strategies and direct the activities of unions to understand the forms of legitimacy and how they can manage them. It would be tempting for officers and union activists to declare that legitimacy does not really matter, that unions are organizations formed for opposition, for fighting the establishment, and that they need only to meet the expectations of members. It would be just as wrong for them to assume that because they themselves see the moral legitimacy of unions—that they personally find the union mission to be of great social value—others will too, and that all that unions need is a good public relations campaign to ensure that this happens. And it would be as wrong for them to assume that when workers join their union, they must be conferring a strong, lasting legitimacy, or that when their union has been certified by a labor board, legitimacy is therefore assured.

The survival of unions depends on their supporters and officers understanding how legitimacy is conferred by constituencies. Unions must not be passive actors. Unions can consciously advance legitimacy in the ways we have mentioned and illustrated with our cases. But to do so, union leaders must understand and appreciate the importance of legitimacy and how and why it is problematic.

They must also understand the relevance of legitimacy to all union activities, from national political lobbying to the organization of the smallest workplaces. Legitimacy is central to gaining critical resources, whether the mobilization of members or the public's or coalition partners' support. For this reason, unions must develop a body of knowledge and experience of working with the concept of legitimacy. This can be done by using others' successful attempts to manage legitimacy as models, for example, borrowing from the Harvard campaign when organizing or from the UPS dispute when striking. And much can be learned by analyzing unsuccessful attempts in terms of their failure to gain pragmatic legitimacy or moral legitimacy or both.

We do not intend this book to be the last word on union legitimacy. What we have done is to propose a new way of thinking about unions—a way that unions themselves neglect at their own peril. We will consider our efforts successful if the concepts we have discussed find their way into research on unions as well as other organizations, are widely considered in unions' strategic decision making, and spur a debate about the unions' value and mission among union supporters and critics. We hope that future discussions of the state of the unions begin with the simple but crucial premise that legitimacy matters.

NOTES

CHAPTER 2 WHO CONFERS LEGITIMACY ON UNIONS?

1. Empirical and historical examinations of union growth are also based on assumptions of union instrumentality. For example, Freeman (1997) devised a model to test the underlying reasons for the spurt in union growth during the Great Depression. He found that union organizing activity rises with union density (the portion of the workforce organized) but falls when density is at high levels. It is less affected by changes in labor laws. His analysis rests largely on changes in employers' estimates of the costs of unionization because of rising density in industrial sectors, the strength of employers' opposition to union organization at very low density levels, and changes in the workers' desire for unionization (given its likely benefits and probable employer opposition).

2. Union instrumentality from the workers' perspective is not a simple economic calculation; rather it can be complex and multifaceted. For example, a related reason for selecting union representation, and one that does not contradict union instrumentality, is the worker's need for involvement in a community. Cornfield et al. (1997) proposed that workers need a sense of community outside the workplace and that this may be satisfied by involvement in community organizations (e.g., church groups, social organizations). Such involvement would preempt union organizing drives. Accordingly, Cornfield and his colleagues hypothesized, the workers least involved in community organizations would be more likely than others to vote for a union in a certification election, all else being equal. This was supported in an analysis of survey data. The authors concluded: "Our study suggests that union organizing should assume that unions can play a broad, social and cultural role in workers' lives. Unions can grow by addressing *not only economic interests* of workers but their interest in community" (Cornfield et al. 1997:258, emphasis added). Community involvement does not diminish the importance of workplace issues (see the data analysis of Cornfield et al. 1997:225), but it does reveal another facet of union instrumentality: providing a sense of community and empowerment through becoming part of an organization that exists outside of work.

Also, instrumentality can be expressed in political as well as workplace terms, that is, the ability of the union to resolve work-related problems through political action. For example, in their survey, Fiorito, Stepina, and Bozeman (1996) found a greater effect for political instrumentality than workplace instrumentality among public sector workers relative to private sector ones. Public sector workers were most concerned about employment security and their unions' ability to affect it politically. The authors concluded that

> consistent with a large body of literature, private sector employees turn to a union because they are unhappy with their jobs and the way that they are treated by their employers. When they feel positively about unions in general and believe unions can be instrumental in improving their employment conditions, a positive vote for unionization results. . . . Public employees believe that unions have significantly less ability to bring change in the workplace and, thus, are not more likely to vote for a union when they are dissatisfied with their jobs. Instead, public employees favor unions when their security is threatened. (Fiorito, Stepina, and Bozeman 1996:475)

3. Both the steel companies and the union were disappointed with the Clinton administration's failure to take strong steps against rising steel imports (i.e., tax breaks for domestic producers) and, once again showing their common objective, jointly asked for legally binding restraints on trade. A bill imposing quotas was passed by the House of Representatives in March 1999 and was proposed to the Senate that month despite the Clinton administration's stated intention to veto such a measure. Steel company executives and the United Steelworkers of America lobbied hard for quotas, claiming that nothing less than the future of the American steel industry was at stake (Adams 1999; Wayne 1999). A bill imposing quotas was defeated in the Senate in June 1999, although legislators did promise to restrict dumping in general (Sanger 1999c). In July 1999 the Clinton administration restricted the import of underpriced steel from Brazil in response to pressure from the coalition of the steel union and domestic steel producers (Sanger 1999a). Preferring to take narrower action, in February 2000 the administration imposed a punitive tariff on steel wire rod and line pipe as part of the anti-dumping measures (Sanger 1999b).

4. In a similar vein, a group of clergy appealed to the administration of St. Vincent Health Systems in Little Rock, Arkansas, to recognize and bargain with a union of nurses. They asked the hospital administrators to "draw on Roman Catholic teaching" and forsake unethical practices of pressuring nurses to reject unionism. Management did not change its tactics, gained a close victory, and, by 1999, faced unfair labor practice charges filed by the union (Francis 1999:8). In recent years there has been an increase in the participation of clergy in coalitions with

unions, primarily because unions seem more often to espouse goals of economic and workplace justice that are similar to religious principles. The clergy show their support through sermons, petitions, pastoral letters, demonstrations, news conferences, and meetings with employers (Greenhouse 1996; 1999a, b; Feingold 1998). In 1999 the National Interfaith Committee for Worker Justice, a coalition of labor and religious leaders, reported that there were about forty-five coalitions devoted to issues of labor and religion; there had been only twelve such coalitions three years earlier (Burkins 1999b). Formal ties between the alliance and the AFL-CIO occur through programs to improve wages and working conditions and lobbying for improved benefits and workplace protections. The coalition could lead to increased union organizing at the grass-roots level, particularly among black and Hispanic immigrants ("Labor, Religion Join Forces" 1999).

5. This is confirmed in a study by Zullo and Eimer (2000) of a union-led coalition of unions and community organizations (Wisconsin Citizen Action), formed in 1996. They found "a remarkable level of diversity in ideological positions between members of the allied organizations" (2000:11). They attribute this diversity to factors related to instrumentality—the partners' sense of political urgency because of the Republican takeover of the Wisconsin state House and Senate two years earlier and the "mutual recognition among key leaders of the need to set aside personal differences and share resources" (2000:11).

6. Ball, Burkins, and White (1999) report some anecdotal evidence of this tendency among workers in the automobile industry.

CHAPTER 3 MANAGING PRAGMATIC LEGITIMACY

1. For a discussion of the Teamsters' communication program to maintain public support and membership solidarity during the UPS strike, see Witt and Wilson (1999).

2. Wolff (1997) believes, however, that a major reason why the public strongly supported the UPS workers was that they valued their personal contact with their local delivery person. This claim, often mentioned in the popular press, is intuitive and quite plausible but not based on any survey data.

3. A year after the strike ended, UPS invoked a contract clause allowing it to nullify the agreement to create full-time jobs. The company claimed the right to do so because the volume of packages shipped had not returned to pre-strike levels, and it needed to lay off rather than hire workers (Blackmon 1998).

4. For the Teamsters' leadership, however, success was short-lived. In March 1997, a federal grand jury began investigating charges that Ron Carey had

received illegal contributions in his 1996 election campaign against James Hoffa Jr. A court-appointed overseer of the Teamsters voided the election on the basis of evidence uncovered in the investigation and later barred Carey from running in the new election. After lengthy legal challenges an election was held in fall 1998, and Hoffa's party defeated a slate of candidates associated with Carey (Greenhouse 1998b).

5. A revealing comparison can be made between the UPS strike and the strike of the United Automobile Workers against General Motors in the summer of 1998. The GM strike began at two plants as the union reacted to the company's outsourcing of the work of union members who made stamping dies. It lasted for fifty days and involved 150,000 workers at its peak. Lost production for GM was estimated at $1 billion. In the end, the company backed off transferring the work. A post mortem on the strike concluded that it "never captured the public's attention in the way the United Parcel strike did." The UPS strike was used by the labor movement as a "rallying cry to tell nonunion workers there was a reason to join a union," but the GM strike, focusing on local issues and seeking to save high-paying jobs, was seen by many as "yet another example of some Brahmins of blue collar labor biting the hand that feeds them." The UAW leaders did a "poor job framing the issues to win public backing for the strikers" (Greenhouse 1998a:D5).

6. The first major field test of the group benefits approach was held in Cincinnati in 1988 with the creation of the National Association of Working Americans (NAWA), a group that described itself as:

> a membership organization sponsored by the Cincinnati AFL-CIO Labor Council for people in the Tri-State Area [i.e., Ohio, Kentucky, and Indiana] who do not have a union where they work, and for people who are unemployed, working part-time, self employed or retired. . . . NAWA is a voice of action on issues critical to working men and women and their families such as health care, family leave, and workplace and environmental safety. NAWA and its members work closely with the Cincinnati AFL-CIO Labor Council and its unions and with community organizations throughout the Greater Cincinnati area. (National Association of Working Americans, n.d. b:1)

NAWA's recruiting brochures emphasized its benefits program: a subscription to the bimonthly newsletter *On the Job*, discounted visits to an occupational health center and local hospitals, the right to apply for the AFL-CIO Mastercard, low-interest home mortgages, group term life insurance, discounted shopping, low-cost prescription drugs, a legal aid program, and a call-in hotline for questions about workplace problems. Annual membership dues were $20. The NAWA project, which lasted from 1988 to 1992, received a poor response to its mailings—about 1 percent (National Association of Working Americans n.d. a, b).

7. For an analysis of the other forms of associate membership specified in union constitutions, see Sherer and Leblebici (1990). The most basic and prevalent form of associate membership program—the one discussed in this chapter—provides group benefits to individuals who affiliate with unions at rates less than the usual dues. Associate membership has also been used by some unions to form ties with immigrant workers and provide help with immigration regulations, English courses, and enforcement of minimum wage and job safety regulations. A primary objective is to create solidarity and union awareness among these workers for future organizing for collective bargaining. In addition, associate membership programs formed by unions and the AFL-CIO on regional bases have been used to lobby for protective labor legislation through coalitions with unions and human rights organizations (Milbank 1993). In 1991 the AFL-CIO claimed that its affiliates had 300,000 associate members (about 2 percent of total membership); most, however, were not members of group benefit plans but public sector employees who had opted not to join the union at their workplace but paid dues and fees as associate members (Northrup 1991).

8. Accordingly, the *AFL-CIO News* published an article by Medoff and Mendelson (1985) that showed how the earliest unions were benevolent societies based on providing mutual aid and insurance rather than collective bargaining.

9. Critics believed not only that offering associate membership through group benefits was wrong in itself but also that it diminished union bargaining power by attracting members who are not represented in negotiations and would not go on strike alongside regular union members. Associate membership would also hinder unions' efforts to organize their industry or craft more fully. And local officers were concerned that the national union headquarters would recruit associate members and provide benefits for them, lessening the importance and funding of union locals (Apcar 1985; Ichniowski and Zax 1990; Lawler 1990).

For additional reasons, construction unions strongly opposed associate member status. Construction work differs from manufacturing work because the product stays and the workers move on at the completion of each job. Because of this, workers feel a greater attachment to their union than to the union-management relationship. The bond between union and member occurs primarily outside the workplace and the collective agreement. Because of these circumstances, union officers feared that associate membership would tempt workers to reject regular membership, and the payment of full dues, when they were between jobs (Jarley and Fiorito 1990; Fiorito and Jarley 1992). Moreover, regular union members were concerned that associate members would compete with them over access to jobs at unionized projects ("Trades Cool to Plan" 1985: Stone and Gallagher 1997).

10. Another reason for the low priority on group benefits programs for associate members might be the tax implications. In 1996, in *National League of Postmasters v. Commissioner*, the U.S. Court of Appeals for the Fourth Circuit affirmed a decision by the U.S. Tax Court concerning the postmasters union's collection of dues from associate members, who were entitled to purchase health insurance, group legal services, and a newsletter. It found that the union's activities with respect to these special members were not conducted in a way that was substantively related to its tax-exempt purpose of improving their working conditions. IRS rules, however, do not treat union dues as unrelated business income, and thus taxable, unless associate membership has been formed or made use of primarily to produce such income. The purpose of associate membership is determined by the union, not the member. Jacobs and Goedert's (1997) review of the doctrine finds it to be quite vague, and they suggest that those organizations whose associate members have less than full voting rights may have to document the participation of associate members in the tax-exempt work of the union. Otherwise, it could be construed that associate members' dues constitute marketing fees. There is no evidence, however, that tax implications were a primary reason for the unions to place a low priority on group benefits programs for associate members. It is noteworthy that the IRS published its technical advice memorandum about associate membership in 1993, and the Court of Appeals affirmed the U.S. Tax Court decision in 1996, both well after the 1985 AFL-CIO report encouraging associate membership and the unions' generally unsuccessful experimentation with the option.

CHAPTER 4 GAINING MORAL LEGITIMACY

1. Canadian unions also opposed NAFTA, while the Mexican unions were neutral or supported it in the hope that jobs would be created in Mexico and because of their close ties with the government.

2. Normally only the Senate ratifies treaties, including trade agreements, but when Congress passed fast track authority for the NAFTA negotiations, the House of Representatives also gained the right to consider the pact. Proponents of fast track argued that other countries would not negotiate trade matters with the United States if agreements were subject to numerous revisions as Congress tried to satisfy special interest groups. Fast track authority was enacted in 1974, but efforts to renew it failed in 1995. The Clinton administration did not propose it again in 1996 because it was considered too divisive an issue to raise before the election. A fast track proposal was blocked by a union-led coalition in 1997 (Sanger 1997).

3. For a review, comparison, and evaluation of the environmental and labor side agreements to NAFTA, see Housman and Orbuch (1993) and de Mastral (1998).

4. Massive job losses as a result of NAFTA's passage were widely predicted, but the actual impact is unclear. Some reports estimated losses ranging from 125,000 to 600,000 American jobs by 1997 because of U.S. investment in and imports from Mexico and Canada. But others found gains of over 300,000 jobs (Harbrecht 1993; Bureau of National Affairs 1997; Hecker 1997; Lawrence 1997; McGinn 1997; Weintraub 1997, 1999). One analyst concluded, "We have heard neither a giant sucking sound nor the boom of a job explosion" (Wheeler 1997:247). The government's claim that trade with Mexico would be a boon to the economy proved to be an exaggeration. By mid-1997 there was an estimated gain of 90,000 to 160,000 new American jobs resulting from increased trade with Mexico under the pact, but this was hardly a significant figure compared to the more than 13 million new jobs created in the booming American economy since the passage of NAFTA (Mitchell 1997). Moreover, as other analysts have noted,

> it is difficult, if not impossible, to disentangle the separate effects of agreements like NAFTA from the myriad of other interrelated forces that are occurring at the same time and that may be induced in part by factors such as NAFTA. These interrelated forces include technological change, global competition in general, other trade liberalization agreements[,] . . . industrial restructuring (especially from manufacturing to services in Canada and the United States), deregulation and privatization, prolonged recessions and macro-economic instability. (Verma et al. 1996:437–438)

Apart from actual gains and losses of jobs, NAFTA did make employers' threats of plant relocation viable, giving them the upper hand in bargaining and a way to dissuade workers from supporting unions during organizing drives (Koech-lin 1995). Also, the value of the labor agreement remains a contentious issue (see, for example, Verma et al. 1996; Adams and Singh 1997; Hecker 1997; de Mastral 1998; and DePalma 1998). In one way, the side agreement made the unions winners because it established an important precedent. This was the first time that a trade agreement has been closely linked to labor issues (Hecker 1997). But the unions believe that the agreement has not discouraged Mexican employers from interfering with the rights of their workers to unionize or vio-lating safety and health standards at their workplaces (e.g., Shields 1995; Cook et al. 1997; Shorrock 1997). Supporters of the labor side agreement contend, however, that it was never intended to punish companies for their labor prac-tices, or to create common labor standards in North America. The goal of trade agreements, Charlene Barsnefsky, the U.S. chief trade negotiator, claimed, is to open rapidly growing markets to America exports; "it is not realistic to suggest that countries will rewrite their domestic labor and environmental laws for the privilege of buying more of our goods" (Mitchell 1997:A24).

5. The coalition's role was an important factor but by no means the only one in the defeat of fast track in 1997. Schoch (1998) believes that this time labor's success was possible, in contrast to its earlier loss on NAFTA, because of changes in public and expert opinion about extending trade, weaker support by business and the Clinton administration, and greater opposition by Republi-cans and, most important, from Democrats as well. Significantly, the Democ-rats' increased opposition resulted from their increased dependence on union funds for their election campaigns and pressure from labor's, and its coalition partners', well-coordinated campaign.

6. The unions' hand in trade matters was further strengthened when they endorsed Al Gore in the 1999–2000 Democratic presidential primary, encour-aging Gore and President Clinton to espouse openly the unions' goal of making labor issues part of trade negotiations (Kahn 2000a). At the winter 2000 meet-ing of the AFL-CIO, the federation announced its Campaign for Global Fair-ness, an effort to have sanctions made part of trade agreements so they could be imposed against countries that violate labor standards such as bans on child la-bor and the protection of workers' rights to organize (Burkins and Cooper 2000). Such standards were included in a 2000 trade agreement between the United States and Jordan (Kahn 2000b). Critics of the unions' new role and militancy in trade matters have argued that the unions' motive is to protect their members rather than help workers in developing countries (Friedman 2000a, b; Kahn 2000b). For example, Friedman (2000b:A31) writes: "This coali-

tion [against free trade] is supported by U.S. unions that have launched a protectionist jihad against free trade with the developing world, for fear of competition. The unions don't want to say that out loud—so they tell you that they are for free trade with countries that get their worker standards up."

7. Nurses account for about one-quarter of the typical hospital's labor force and its single largest labor cost ("More Nursing Care" 1998).

8. For a review of early bargaining by nurses and related labor laws, see Flanagan (1983). From 1935 to 1947, all employees of private hospitals, whether or not they were operated for profit, were protected in their right to bargain by labor law (i.e., the National Labor Relations Act). They were, however, excluded under the 1947 Labor-Management Relations Act. In ensuing years, nurses and other health care workers gained protected rights to bargain under twelve state laws, including one in Massachusetts. Under the 1974 amendments to federal labor laws, coverage was extended to private nonprofit hospitals nationally (Flanagan 1983:4–7).

9. After the passage of the Health Care Amendments, employers pressed for broad bargaining units in representation cases to increase the chances of union defeat in a heterogeneous group without a clear community of interest, and to make bargaining less frequent if certification did occur. There were no established standards for appropriate bargaining units in the health care industry, and hearings for certification petitions before the labor board were often long and contentious. But in the aftermath of a series of landmark cases regarding health care units (*St. Francis Hospital* 265 NLRB 220, 271 NLRB 160, 814 F.2nd 697 and 286 NLRB 123), the labor board agreed to a rule identifying eight potentially appropriate bargaining units: physicians, registered nurses, other professional employees (e.g., pharmacists), technical employees (e.g., LPNs, lab technicians), skilled maintenance workers, business office clericals, other nonprofessional and service employees, and guards. The board considered these to be commonly found employee groups that would have separate representation if, at a work site, they actually possessed a separate community of interest. For a brief review of the evolution and implications of the *St. Francis* decision and related board decision making, see Feldacker (2000:49–51) and Hirsch and Schumacher (1998:136–141). The creation of separate units for registered nurses increased the likelihood of their successful unionization and made their organizing more attractive to nurses' associations and health care unions (Lippman 1991).

10. Seventeen percent of respondents in a survey of hospital administrators reported union organizing among nurses between January and June 1998, up from 14 percent a year earlier (Rockey 1999).

11. Of the 120,000 nurses in Massachusetts, 80,000 were eligible to be covered by collective bargaining. The rate of unionization was 23 percent (19,000 nurses)—one of the highest rates in the country (Goldstein 1998). Nationally, 17 percent of the 2.2 million registered nurses were union members (Greene 1998).

12. The UAPs' level of training depends on the hospital. A study of hospitals in California found that "99 percent . . . provided their aides with fewer than 120 hours of on-the-job training. Fifty-nine percent offered fewer than 20 hours of classroom instruction. Only 1 in 5 of the state's hospitals required aides to have a high school diploma" (Gordon 1997).

13. Indeed, there is support for the use of RNs rather than less skilled staff in a study by the U.S. Department of Health and Human Services. Researchers found that the more hours worked by RNs at selected hospitals, the fewer the complications after surgery in conditions sensitive to nursing care (e.g., urinary tract infections) ("More Nursing Care" 1998).

14. The positive relationship between nurses' concerns about threats to patient care and their propensity to unionize is supported in a study by Clark et al. (1999).

REFERENCES

Adams, Chris. 1999. "Steel Companies, Union Criticize U.S. Import Plan." *Wall Street Journal,* January 11, A6.

Adams, Roy J. 1989. "North American Industrial Relations: Divergent Trends in Canada and the United States." *International Labor Review* 12 (January–February): 47–64.

———. 1995. *Industrial Relations under Liberal Democracy.* Columbia: University of South Carolina Press.

Adams, Roy J., and Parbudyal Singh. 1997. "Early Experience with NAFTA's Labour Side Accord." *Comparative Labor Law Journal* 18 (winter): 161–181.

AFL-CIO. 1985. *The Changing Situation of Workers and Their Unions.* Washington, D.C.: AFL-CIO.

———. 1992. "International Trade: Where We Stand." Fact sheet accompanying program for the Trade for the Twenty-first Century conference, September 8–10, Washington, D.C.

———. 1998. "Speech of President John Sweeney." www.aflcio.org/publ/speech98/pres.

AFL-CIO Executive Council. 1993. "Statement by the AFL-CIO Executive Council on the North American Free Trade Agreement," February 17, Bal Harbor, Fla.

AFL-CIO Task Force on Trade. 1993. *Action Source Book.* Washington, D.C.: AFL-CIO.

Ahlén, Kristina. 1992. "Union Legitimacy: Members' Perceptions of Union Government." Paper presented at the Symposium on Emerging Union Structures: An International Comparison, March 9, Clark University, Worcester, Mass.

———. 1995. "Democratic Legitimacy in Swedish Labor Unions: The Role of Instrumentality in Forming Members' Perceptions." In *Changing Employment Relations: Behavioral and Social Perspectives,* edited by Lois E. Tetrick and Julian Barling. Washington, D.C.: American Psychological Association. 209–227.

Aldrich, Howard E., and C. Marlene Fiol. 1994. "Fools Rush In? The Institutional Context of Industry Creation." *Academy of Management Review* 19 (December): 645–670.

Alexander, Jeffrey A., and Thomas A. D'Aunno. 1990. "Transformation of Institutional Environments: Perspectives on the Corporatization of U.S. Health Care." In *Innovations in Health Care Delivery: New Insights into Organization Theory*, edited by Stephen Mick. San Francisco: Jossey Bass. 53–85.

Apcar, Leonard M. 1985. "AFL-CIO's Novel Program to Expand Union Membership Meets Resistance." *New York Times*, October 30, 7.

Ashforth, Blake E., and Barrie W. Gibbs. 1990. "The Double Edge of Organizational Legitimation." *Organization Science* 1 (2): 177–194.

Atanassov, Bayko. 1995. "Emerging Union Structures in Bulgaria: Two Aspects of Legitimacy." Paper presented at the Second International Conference on Emerging Union Structures, June 14, Stockholm.

Audley, John. 1993. "Why Environmentalists Are Angry about the North American Free Trade Agreement." In *Trade and the Environment: Laws, Economics, and Policy*, edited by Durwood Zaelke, Paul Orbuch, and Robert F. Housman. Washington, D.C.: Island Press. 191–202.

Baker, Gerard. 1997. "Big Labor, Big Fightback." *Financial Times*, September 29, 19.

Ball, Jeffrey, Glenn Burkins and Gregory White. 1999. "Don't Walk: Why Labor Unions Are Reluctant to Use the 'S' Word." *Wall Street Journal*, December 16, A1, A8.

Bamberger, Peter A., Avraham N. Kluger, and Ronena Suchard. 1999. "The Antecedents and Consequences of Union Commitment: A Meta-analysis." *Academy of Management Journal* 42 (June): 304–318.

Barbash, Jack. 1987. "Like Nature, Industrial Relations Abhors a Vacuum." *Relations Industrielles* 42 (1): 3–27.

Barkin, Solomon. 1986. "The Current Unilateralist Counterattack on Unionism and Collective Bargaining." *Relations Industrielles* 41 (1): 3–27.

Barling, Julian, Clive Fullagar, and E. Kevin Kelloway. 1992. *The Union and Its Members: A Psychological Approach*. New York: Oxford University Press.

Behr, Peter. 1993a. "Clinton's Conversion on NAFTA." *Washington Post*, September 19, H1, H4.

———. 1993b. "NAFTA Creating Odd Alliance." *Washington Post*, September 4, A1, A14–A15.

———. 1993c. "NAFTA Friends and Foes Have Different Views of U.S. Economic Strengths." *Washington Post*, September 15, D1, D3.

Berger, C. J., C. Olson, and J. W. Boudreau. 1983. "Effects of Unions on Job Satisfaction: The Role of Work-Related Values and Perceived Rewards." *Organizational Behavior and Human Performance* 32 (December): 289–324.

Blackmon, Douglas A. 1998. "UPS Nullifies Part of Teamster Contract." *Wall Street Journal*, July 10, A3, A8.

Brett, Jeanne M. 1980. "Why Employees Want Unions." *Organizational Dynamics* 8 (spring): 47–59.

Bronfenbrenner, Kate. 1998. "Reversing the Tide of Organizing Decline: Lessons from the U.S. Experience." *New Zealand Journal of Industrial Relations* 23 (2): 21–34.

Bureau of National Affairs. 1997. "Administration Report Says NAFTA Has Had Modest Positive Impact." *Labor Relations Week*, July 16, 745.

——. 1999. "Whistle Blowers Protections in Massachusetts Budget." *Weekly Labor Report*, June 14, 628.

Burgoon, Brian. 1995. "NAFTA Thoughts: Evaluating Labor's Fair Trade Strategy." *Dollars and Sense* (September–October): 10–13, 40.

Burkins, Glenn. 1999a. "Work Week." *Wall Street Journal*, April 20, A1.

——. 1999b. "Work Week." *Wall Street Journal*, August 10, A1.

——. 2000. "Labor Union Membership Increases Second Year in Row to 16.48 Million." *Wall Street Journal*, January 20, A2.

Burkins, Glenn, and Helene Cooper. 2000. "Union Ad Blitz Aims at China and WTO." *Wall Street Journal*, February 17, A2.

Carlson, Richard R. 1992. "The Origin and Future of Exclusive Representation in American Labor Law." *Duquesne Law Review* 30 (summer): 779–867.

Chaison, Gary N., and Dileep G. Dhavale. 1990. "A Note on the Severity of the Decline in Union Organizing." *Industrial and Labor Relations Review* 43 (April): 366–373.

——. 1992. "The Choice between Union Membership and Free-Rider Status." *Journal of Labor Research* (fall): 355–369.

Chaison, Gary N., and Joseph B. Rose. 1991. "The Macro-determinants of Union Growth and Decline." In *The State of the Unions,* edited by George Strauss, Daniel Gallagher, and Jack Fiorito. Madison, Wisc.: Industrial Relations Research Association. 3–45.

Chaison, Gary N., Barbara Bigelow, and Edward Ottensmeyer. 1993. "Unions and Legitimacy: A Conceptual Refinement." In *Research in the Sociology of Organizations,* edited by Samuel B. Bacharach, Ronald Seeber, and David Walsh. Greenwich, Conn.: JAI Press. 139–166.

"The Changing Role of Nurses: For Some Health Care Is Changing Too Rapidly." 1997. *Sunday Enterprise* (Brockton, Mass.), March 30, 1.

Clark, Paul F., Darlene A. Clark, David Day, and Dennis Shea. 1999. "Health Care Reform's Impact on Hospitals: Implementations for Union Organizing."

Proceedings of the Fifty-first Annual Meeting of the Industrial Relations Research Association. Madison, Wisc.: IRRA. 61–67.

Clymer, Adam. 2000. "House Vote on China Trade: The Politics Was Local." *New York Times,* May 27, A3.

Collective Bargaining Forum. 1999. "Principles for New Employment Relationships: The Collective Bargaining Forum." *Perspective on Work* 3 (1): 32–39.

Cook, Maria Lorena, Morley Gunderson, Mark Thompson, and Anil Verma. 1997. "Making Free Trade More Fair: Developments in Protecting Labor Rights." *Labor Law Journal* 48 (August): 519–529.

Cooper, Helene. 2000. "Clinton Moves to Impose Punitive Tariffs on Imports in Some Steel Industries." *Wall Street Journal,* February 14, A36.

Cornfield, Daniel. 1999. "Shifts in Public Approval of Labor Unions in the United States, 1936–1999." *Gallup Guest Scholar Poll Review,* September 2, www.gallup.com.

Cornfield, Dan, Holly McCammon, Darren McDaniel, and Dean Eatman. 1997. "In the Community of the Union? The Impact of Community Involvement on Nonunion Worker Attitudes about Unionizing." In *Organizing to Win: New Research on Union Strategies,* edited by Kate Bronfenbrenner et al. Ithaca: Cornell University Press. 245–248.

Council of the Americas. 1993. *Washington Report* (fall issue). Washington, D.C.: Council of the Americas.

Cowie, Jefferson. 1997. "National Struggles in Transnational Economy: A Critical Analysis of U.S. Labor's Campaign against NAFTA." *Labor Studies Journal* 21 (winter): 2–32.

Craft, James A., and Marion M. Extejt. 1983. "New Strategies in Union Organizing." *Journal of Labor Research* 4 (winter): 19–32.

Craven, Bill. 1998. "California Sierra Club Opposes Proposition 226." Sierra Club press release, May 19.

Craypo, Charles, and Bruce Nissen. 1993. "The Impact of Corporate Strategies." In *Grand Designs: The Impact of Corporate Strategies on Workers, Unions, and Communities,* edited by Charles Craypo and Bruce Nissen. Ithaca: Cornell University Press. 224–250.

Cutcher-Gershenfeld, Joel. 1984. "Labor-Management Cooperation in American Communities: What's in It for Unions?" *Annals of the American Academy of Political and Social Science* 473 (May): 76–87.

Cutcher-Gershenfeld, Joel, Thomas A. Kochan, and John Calhoun Wells. 1998. "How Do Labor and Management View Collective Bargaining." *Monthly Labor Review* 121 (October): 23–31.

Davis, Bob. 1992. "Fighting NAFTA: Free-Trade Pact Spurs a Diverse Coalition of Grass Roots Foes." *Wall Street Journal,* December 23, A1–A6.

Delaney, John T. 1998. "Redefining the Right-to-Work Debate: Unions and the Dilemma of Free Choice." *Journal of Labor Research* (summer): 425–443.

De Mastral, A. L. C. 1998. "The Significance of the NAFTA Side Agreements on Environmental and Labor Cooperation." *Arizona Journal of International and Comparative Law* 15 (1): 169–185.

DePalma, Anthony. 1998. "Canadians Raise Concerns about Mexican Labor Laws." *New York Times,* November 25, C2.

Deshpande, Satish P., and Jack Fiorito. 1989. "Specific and General Beliefs in Union Voting Models." *Academy of Management Journal* 32 (December): 883–897.

Donahue, Thomas R. 1993a. "Statement of Thomas R. Donahue." *North American Free Trade Agreement: Affects* [sic] *on Workers: Hearing of the Committee on Labor and Human Resources, United States Senate,* October 13. Washington, D.C.: U.S. Government Printing Office. 44–48.

———. 1993b. "Statement of Thomas R. Donahue." *North American Free Trade Agreement (NAFTA) and Supplemental Agreements to NAFTA: Hearings before the Committee on Ways and Means and Its Subcommittee on Trade, U.S. House of Representatives,* September 14, 15, 21, and 23, 1993. Washington, D.C.: U.S. Government Printing Office. 511–515.

Dowling, John, and Jeffrey Pfeffer. 1975. "Organizational Legitimacy: Social Values and Organizational Behavior." *Pacific Sociological Review* 18 (1): 122–136.

Edsall, Thomas B. 1993. "Split over NAFTA May Strengthen Force of Disaffected Voters." *Washington Post,* November 19, A39.

Edwards, Richard, and Michael Podgursky. 1986. "The Unraveling Accord: American Unions in Crisis." In *Unions in Crisis and Beyond: Perspectives from Six Countries,* edited by Richard Edwards, Paolo Garonna, and Franz Todtling. Dover, Mass.: Auburn House. 14–60.

Fantasia, Rick. 1988. *Cultures of Solidarity: Consciousness, Action, and Contemporary American Workers.* Berkeley: University of California Press.

Farber, Henry S. 1987. "The Recent Decline of Unionization in the United States." *Science* 238 (November 13): 915–920.

Feingold, Danny. 1998. "Putting Faith in Labor: In a New Trend, a Motley Coalition of Southland Clergy Is Taking Up the Workers' Cause—and Winning." Online posting of *Los Angeles Times* article, August 28, labnews@cmsa.berkeley.edu.

Feldacker, Bruce. 2000. *Labor Guide to Labor Laws.* 4th ed. Upper Saddle River, N.J.: Prentice Hall.

"Finding Their Voice: Kris Rondeau Discusses Organizing with Richard Balzer." 1993. *Boston Review* 18 (October–November): 1–3.

Fiorito, Jack, and Paul Jarley. 1992. "Associate Membership Programs: Innovation and Diversification in National Unions." *Academy of Management Journal* 35 (5): 1070–85.

Fiorito, Jack, Paul Jarley, and John Thomas Delaney. 1993. "National Union Effectiveness." *Research in the Sociology of Organizations* 12: 111–137.

Fiorito, Jack, Lee P. Stepina, and Dennis P. Bozeman. 1996. "Explaining the Unionism Gap: Public-Private Sector Differences in Preferences for Unionization." *Journal of Labor Research* 17 (summer): 463–478.

Flanagan, Lydia. 1983. *Collective Bargaining and the Nursing Profession.* Kansas City, Mo.: American Nurses Association.

"Foreign Steel Is Being Dumped at Cutthroat Prices." 1998. *New York Times,* September 17, A18.

Francis, Theo. 1999. "St. Vincent Union Vote Deadlocks." *Little Rock Arkansas Democrat-Gazette,* November 5, 1, 8.

Freeman, Richard B. 1989. "What Does the Future Hold for U.S. Unionism?" *Relations Industrielles* 44 (winter): 25–43.

———. 1997. *Spurts in Union Growth: Defining Movements and Social Processes.* NBER Working Paper Series, no. 6012. Cambridge, Mass.: National Bureau of Economic Research.

Freeman, Richard B., and Joel Rogers. 1993. "Who Speaks for US?: Employee Representation in a Nonunion Labor Market." In *Employee Representation: Alternatives and Future Directions,* edited by Bruce Kaufman and Morris M Kleiner. Madison, Wisc.: Industrial Relations Research Association. 13–79.

———. 1994a. *Worker Representation and Participation Survey: Report on the Findings.* Princeton: Survey Research Associates.

———. 1994b. *Worker Representation and Participation Survey: First Report on the Findings.* Princeton: Survey Research Associates.

———. 1999. *What Workers Want.* Ithaca: Cornell University Press.

Friedman, Thomas. 2000a. "1 Davos, 3 Seattle." *New York Times,* February 1, A25.

———. 2000b. "Parsing the Protests." *New York Times,* April 14, A31.

Fullagar, Clive, Renee Slick, Conan Sumer, and Paul Marquardt. 1997. "Union Attitudes, Ideologues, and Instrumentalists." In *The Future of Trade Unionism: International Perspectives on Emerging Union Structures,* edited by Magnus Sverke. Aldershot: Ashgate. 263–276.

Gahan, Peter, and Simon Bell. 1999. "Union Strategy, Membership Orientation and Union Effectiveness: An Exploratory Analysis." *Labour & Industry* 9 (April): 5–28.

"Gallup/CNN/*USA Today* Poll." 1998. *Polling Report*, November 18, www. gallup.com.

Gallup Organization. 1997. *Gallup Poll Archives, 1997*, www.gallup.com/poll_archives/1997.

Garland, Susan. 1993. "The Unions vs. Pro-NAFTA Democrats: Get Over It." *Business Week* 3749 (December 6): 45.

Gold, Charlotte. 1986. *Labor-Management Committees: Confrontation, Cooptation, or Cooperation.* Ithaca: ILR Press.

Golden, Tim. 1993. "Mexicans Roiling with Anger at Perot's Depiction of Them." *New York Times,* November 11, A1, A22.

Goldstein, Myrna Chandler. 1998. "From Evolution to Revolution: As Nursing Changes, Many Turn to Unions." *Hospital News Massachusetts* 15 (May): 1, 7–9.

Gonzalez, Jennifer. 1999. "Registered Nurses at Health Partners Join Union." *Cleveland Plain Dealer,* May 8, 2B.

Goodman-Draper, Jacqueline. 1995. *Health Care's Forgotten Majority: Nurses and Their Frayed White Collars.* Westport, Conn.: Auburn House.

Gordon, Suzanne. 1997. "Nurses, Like Patients, Pay for Hospital Changes: Financial Pressures Squeeze Hospital Staff, and May Jeopardize Patient Care." *Boston Sunday Globe,* March 2, D2.

Greene, Jan. 1998. "Labor Groups Look to Nursing to Boost Their Dwindling Ranks, Promising Tough Tactics." *Hospital and Health Networks* 72 (June): 38–39.

Greenfield, Patricia A., and Robert J. Pleasure. 1993. "Representatives of Their Own Choosing: Finding Workers' Voice in the Legitimacy and Power of Their Unions." In *Employee Representation,* edited by Bruce E. Kaufman and Morris M. Kleiner. Madison, Wisc.: Industrial Relations Research Association. 169–196.

Greenhouse, Steven. 1996a. "Despite Setbacks, Labor Chief Is Upbeat over Election Role." *New York Times,* November 15, A20.

——. 1996b. "Labor and Clergy Reunite to Help Society's Underdogs." *New York Times,* August 18, A1, A45.

——. 1997a. "Teamsters Get Public Support." *New York Times,* August 17, A1, A28.

——. 1997b. "United Parcel Pension Plan Puts Teamster Leader in Tight Spot." *New York Times,* August 14, A1, A28.

——. 1997c. "UPS Says Fears of Bigger Losses Made It Cut Deal." *New York Times,* August 20, A1, A22.

———. 1997d. "Why Labor Feels It Can't Afford to Lose This Strike." *New York Times*, August 17, E3.

———. 1997e. "Yearlong Effort Key to Success for Teamsters." *New York Times*, August 25, A1, A15.

———. 1998a. "Hoffa Will Lead Teamsters after Chief Rival Concedes." *New York Times*, December 6, 1, 36.

———. 1998b. "For the UAW, Huge Price and Tiny Victory at G.M." *New York Times*, July 30, D5.

———. 1999a. "A.F.L.-C.I.O. Plans $40 Million Political Drive." *New York Times*, February 18, A19.

———. 1999b. "Clergy and Unions Teaming up Again." *New York Times*, September 6, A9.

———. 1999c. "Long-time Foes Join to Promote Jobs and Earth." *New York Times*, October 4, A12.

———. 2000a. "Labor Is Ready to Fight Easing of China Trade." *New York Times*, December 3, A1, A12.

———. 2000b. "Unions Deny Stand over Trade Is Protectionism." *New York Times*, April 24, A1, A9.

Greenhouse, Steven, and Joseph Kahn. 1999. "U.S. Effort to Add Labor Standards to Agenda Fails." *New York Times*, December 3, A1, A12.

Gross, James A. 1994. "The Demise of the National Labor Policy: A Question of Social Justice." In *Restoring the Promise of American Labor Law*, edited by Sheldon Friedman, Richard W. Hurd, Rudolph A. Oswald, and Ronald Seeber. Ithaca: Cornell University Press. 45–58.

Hammel, Lee. 1998. "St. Vincent Registered Nurses Vote for Union." *Worcester Telegram & Gazette*, February 6, 1.

Harbrecht, Douglas. 1993. "NAFTA: Con—A Jobs Nightmare." *Business Week* 3336 (September 13): 26–28.

Harbridge, Raymond, and Anthony Honeybone. 1996. "External Legitimacy of Unions: Trends in New Zealand." *Journal of Labor Research* 17 (summer): 425–444.

Harvard Union of Clerical and Technical Workers. N.d. *Speaking for Ourselves, Making a Difference*. Cambridge, Mass.: HUCTW.

"Health-Care Squeeze Speeds Unionization." *The Berkshire Eagle* (January 31): 1.

Heath, Rebecca. 1998. "The New Working Class." *American Demographics* 20 (January): 51–55.

Hecker, JayEtta Z. 1997. *North American Free Trade Agreement: Impacts and Implementation: Testimony before the Subcommittee on Trade, Committee on*

Ways and Means, House of Representatives. Washington, D.C.: U.S. General Accounting Office.

Heckscher, Charles. 1988. *The New Unionism*. New York: Basic Books.

Heckscher, Charles, and David Palmer. 1993. "Associational Movements and Employment Rights: An Emerging Paradigm?" In *Research in the Sociology of Organizations*, edited by Samuel Bacharach, Ronald Seeber, and David Walsh. Greenwich, Conn.: JAI Press. 279–309.

Heshizer, Brian, and John Lund. 1997. "Union Commitment Types and Union Activist Involvement: Lessons for Union Organizers and Labor Educators?" *Labor Studies Journal* 22 (June): 66–76.

Hirsch, Barry T., and Edward J. Schumacher. 1998. "Union Wages, Rents, and Skills in Health Care Labor Markets." *Journal of Labor Research* 19 (winter): 125–147.

Hoerr, John. 1997. *We Can't Eat Prestige: The Women Who Organized Harvard*. Philadelphia: Temple University Press.

Housman, Robert F., and Paul M. Orbuch. 1993. "Integrating Labor and Environmental Concerns in the North American Free Trade Agreement: A Look Back and a Look Ahead." *American University Journal of International Law and Policy* 8 (summer): 719–815.

"HUCTW Ratifies Agreement to Extend Contract." 1998. *Harvard University Gazette*, March 12, www.harvard.edu/gazette.

Hufbauer, Gary Clyde, and Jeffrey J. Schott. 1993. *NAFTA: An Assessment*. Washington, D.C.: Institute for International Economics.

Hurd, Richard D. 1993. "Organizing and Representing Clerical Workers: The Harvard Model." In *Women and Unions: Forging a Partnership*, edited by Dorothy Sue Cobble. Ithaca: ILR Press. 316–348.

Ichniowski, Casey, and Jeffrey S. Zax. 1990. "Today's Associations, Tomorrow's Unions." *Industrial and Labor Relations Review* 43 (January): 191–208.

Irwin, Douglas A. 1999. "How Clinton Botched the Seattle Summit." *Wall Street Journal*, December 6, A34.

Jacobs, Jerald A., and Paula Cozzi Goedert. 1997. "Associate Members Dues: Still a Concern." *Association Management* 49 (June): 137, 143.

Jarley, Paul, and Jack Fiorito. 1990. "Associate Membership: Unionism or Consumerism." *Industrial and Labor Relations Review* 43 (January): 209–224.

Jarley, Paul, and Sarosh Kuruvilla. 1994. "American Trade Unions and Public Approval: Can Unions Please All of the People All of the Time?" *Journal of Labor Research* 15 (spring): 97–116.

Jepperson, Ronald L. 1991. "Institutions, Institutional Effects, and Institutionalism." In *The New Institutionalism in Organizational Analysis*, edited by Walter

W. Powell and Paul J. DiMaggio. Chicago: University of Chicago Press. 143–163.

Kahn, Joseph. 2000a. "Clinton Shift on Trade: 'Wake-Up Call.' " *New York Times,* January 31, A6.

———. 2000b. "Labor Praises New Trade Pact with Jordan." *New York Times,* October 25, C1, C12.

Kaufman, Bruce E. 1997. "The Future of the Labor Movement: A Look at the Fundamentals." In *Proceedings of the 1997 Spring Meeting of the Industrial Relations Research Association.* Madison, Wisc.: Industrial Relations Research Association. 474–484.

Ketter, Joni. 1996. *A Seat at the Table: Fifty Years of Progress.* Washington, D.C.: American Nurses Association.

Kirkland, Lane. 1987. "Goal of New Benefit Program: Extend Unionism from Workplace to Marketplace." *AFL-CIO News,* February 14, 1.

Kleiman, Carol. 1997. "Unions Hoping Changes Halt Membership Decline." *Chicago Tribune,* November 30, 6.

Kochan, Leslie. 1989. *The Maquiladoras and Toxics: The Hidden Costs of Production South of the Border.* Washington, D.C.: AFL-CIO.

Kochan, Thomas A. 1988. "Adaptability of the U.S. Industrial Relations System." *Science* 24 (April 15): 287–292.

Kochan, Thomas A., and Harry C. Katz. 1998. *Collective Bargaining and Industrial Relations.* 2d ed. Homewood, Ill.: Irwin.

Kochan, Thomas A., Harry C. Katz, and Robert B. McKersie. 1986. *The Transformation of American Industrial Relations.* New York: Basic Books.

Kochan, Thomas A., Harry C. Katz, and Nancy R. Mower. 1984. *Worker Participation and American Unions: Threat or Opportunity?* Kalamazoo: Upjohn Institute.

Koechlin, Tim. 1995. "NAFTA's Footloose Plants Abandon Workers." *Multinational Monitor* 16 (April): 25–27.

Kunen, James. 1996. "The New Hands-Off Nursing: Are Patients at Risk When Cost-Cutting Hospitals Replace Nurses with 'Technicians' at the Bedside?" *Time* 148 (September 30): 56.

Labor Advisory Committee on the North American Free Trade Agreement. 1992. *Preliminary Report.* Washington, D.C.: Labor Advisory Committee on the North American Free Trade Agreement.

"Labor Letter." 1991. *Wall Street Journal,* February 26, 1.

"Labor, Religion Join Forces in Drive to Reach Grass Roots." 1999. *Worcester Telegram & Gazette,* October 9, B12.

Lahr, Ellen G. 1997a. "Nurses to Take Strike Vote: Day of Decision Comes Monday." *Berkshire Eagle,* May 2, 1, 6.

———. 1997b. "BMC Nurses Stage Rally at Park Square." *Berkshire Eagle,* April 4, A1.

Lasalandra, Michael. 1997. "Nurses Question Care by Aides: Nurses Sick over Use of Unlicensed Workers." *Boston Sunday Herald,* May 11, 1, 8.

Lawler, John J. 1990. *Unionization and Deunionization.* Columbia: University of South Carolina Press.

Lawrence, Richard. 1997. "Nafta Is Confusing Members." *Journal of Commerce,* June 5, 6A.

Leff, Mark. 1997. "UPS Strikers in the U.S. Lead Off Part-Time Workers Protest." CNN World Report, August 10, www.cnnworld.com.

Levinson, Mark. 1997. "Turning Point for Labor." *New York Times,* August 17, E15.

Lewis, Diane, and Alex Pham. 1996. "Nurses at Brigham Authorize a Strike." *Boston Globe,* September 18, A1, A4.

Lichtenstein, Nelson. 1999. "American Trade Unions and the 'Labor Question': Past and Present." In *What's New for Organized Labor?,* edited by Twentieth Century Foundation Task Force on the Future of Unions. New York: Century Foundation Press. 59–117.

Lippman, Helen. 1991. "Expect to Hear about Unions." *RN* 54 (October): 67–69.

Mann, Judy. 1998. "Protecting the Patient by Protecting the Worker." *Washington Post,* August 21, E3.

Massachusetts Nurses Association. 1994a. "MNA Draws Line in Sand over Patient Safety: Plans Public Campaign for Quality Care." *Massachusetts Nurse* 64 (7): 1, 2.

———. 1994b. "Patient Safety Meeting Draws over 200 MNA Members." *Massachusetts Nurse* 64 (9): 1, 2, 7, 16.

———. 1995a. "The MNA SCSC Needs You!" *Massachusetts Nurse* 65 (9): 5.

———. 1995b. "MNA Safe Care Campaign Unveils Consumer Wallet Card: Nurses Urged to Hand Them out to Friends and Neighbors." *Massachusetts Nurse* 65 (5): 12.

———. 1995c. "MNA Hosts Safe Care Town Meeting for Consumer Advocates." *Massachusetts Nurse* 65 (9): 1, 3, 8.

———. 1996a. "Safe Care Town Meeting Draws 23 Consumer Advocacy Groups." *Massachusetts Nurse* 66 (1): 1, 2.

———. 1996b. "MNA Unveils 1996 Legislative Agenda." *Massachusetts Nurse* 66 (1): 1, 4.

———. 1997. "Cape Cod Hospital RNs Ratify Landmark Agreement: Negotiated Nurse Staff Levels Make Pact First of Kind in Massachusetts." *Massachusetts Nurse* 67 (8): 1, 2.

———. 1998a. *MNA Today.* Canton: Massachusetts Nurses Association.

———. 1998b. *1997 Annual Report.* Canton: Massachusetts Nurses Association.

———. 1999a. "An Act Protecting the Conscientious Health Care Employees." Canton: Massachusetts Nurses Association.

———. 1999b. "State Budget Includes Strong Commitment to Improve Health Care and Protect Patients by Supporting Role of Nurses in Health Care Advocacy, Prevention, and Care Delivery." Press release, November 12.

Masters, Marick F. 1997. "Union Wealth: The Bargaining Power Implications." *Journal of Labor Research* 18 (winter): 91–110.

McDonald, Charles J. 1987. "The AFL-CIO's Blueprint for the Future—A Progress Report." *Proceedings of the Thirty-ninth Annual Meeting of the Industrial Relations Research Association.* Madison, Wisc.: IRRA. 276–282.

McGinn, Chris. 1997. "NAFTA Numbers: Three Years of NAFTA Facts." *Multinational Monitor* 18 (January–February): 31–33.

McMurdy, Deirdre. 1997. "A Two-Tiered Workforce: The UPS Strike Signaled a Growing Push to Improve Conditions for Part-Timers." *Maclean's* 110 (September 1): 48.

Medoff, James L., and Nina A. Mendelson. 1985. "Unions of the Past." *AFL-CIO News,* May 25, 11–12.

Meyer, John W., and Brian Rowan. 1977. "Institutionalized Organizations: Formal Structure as Myth and Ceremony." *American Journal of Sociology* 83 (September): 340–363.

Meyer, John W., and W. Richard Scott. 1983. "Centralization and the Legitimacy Problems of Local Government." In *Organizational Environments,* edited by John W. Meyer and W. Richard Scott. Beverly Hills, Calif.: Sage Publications. 199–215.

Meyer, John W., W. Richard Scott, and Terrence E. Deal. 1983. "Institutional and Technical Sources of Organizational Structure: Explaining the Structure of Educational Organizations." In *Organizational Environments,* edited by John W. Meyer and W. Richard Scott. Beverly Hills, Calif.: Sage Publications. 45–67.

Meyerson, Harold. 1998. "A Second Chance: The New AFL-CIO and the Prospective Revival of American Labor." In *Not Your Father's Union Movement: Inside the AFL-CIO,* edited by Jo-Ann Mort. New York: Verso. 1–26.

Milbank, Dana. 1993. "Labor Broadens Its Appeal by Setting Up Associations to Lobby and Offer Services." *Wall Street Journal,* January 13, B1, B5.

Mitchell, Alison. 1997. "Clinton Faces Off with Congress on Trade." *New York Times,* September 17, A24.

Mitchell, Cynthia. 1998. "The UPS Strike Revisited." *Atlanta Constitution,* August 2, 1.

"The MNA and Nurses: A Purposeful and Effective Synergy." 1998. *MNA Today* (spring): 1.

Moberg, David. 1999. "The U.S. Labor Movement Faces the Twenty-first Century." In *Which Direction for Organized Labor?* edited by Bruce Nissen. Detroit: Wayne State University Press. 21–33.

——. 2000. "Labor Goes Global." *In These Times,* March 20, 12–13.

"More Nursing Care Averts Problems after Surgery, Study Says." 1998. *New York Times,* December 6, 29.

Murray, Alan I., and Yonatan Reshef. 1988. "American Manufacturing Unions' Statis: A Paradigmatic Perspective." *Academy of Management Review* 13 (October): 615–626.

"NAFTA: Who Wins? Who Loses?" 1993. *Washington Post,* November 17, A20.

Nagourney, Adam. 1997. "In the Strike Battle, Teamsters Use Political Tack." *New York Times,* August 16, A1, A8.

National Association of Working Americans. N.d. a. *Because Working Together We Make a Difference.* Cincinnati: National Association of Working Americans.

——. N.d. b. *Membership Benefits.* Cincinnati: National Association of Working Americans.

Newland, Kathleen. 1999. "Workers of the World, Now What?" *Foreign Policy* 114 (spring): 52–65.

Nilsson, Eric A. 1997. "The Growth of Union Decertification: A Test of Two Nonnested Theories." *Industrial Relations* 36 (July): 324–348.

9-to-5—National Association of Working Women. N.d. "Working Women Who Know . . . Take Action." Atlanta: 9-to-5.

Nissen, Bruce. 1995. *Fighting for Jobs: Case Studies of Labor-Community Coalitions Confronting Plant Closings.* Albany: State University of New York Press.

Northrup, Herbert R. 1991. " 'New' Union Approaches to Membership Decline: Reviving the Policies of the 1920s?" *Journal of Labor Research* 12 (fall): 333–347.

Oppenheim, Lisa. 1991. "Women's Way of Organizing: A Conversation with AFSCME Organizers Kris Rondeau and Gladys McKenzie." *Labor Research Review* 18 (fall): 45–59.

Parsons, Talcott. 1960. *Structure and Process in Modern Societies.* Glencoe, Ill.: Free Press.

Perl, Peter. 1985. "Labor Lenders Adopt Blueprint for Change." *Washington Post.* February 22, A4.

Peter D. Hart Research Associates. 1998. "Working Women's View of the Economy, Unions, and Public Policy." In *Not Your Father's Union Movement: Inside the AFL-CIO,* edited by Jo-Ann Mort. New York: Verso. 69–85.

Peters, Ronald, and Theresa Merrill. 1997. "Clergy and Religious Persons' Roles in Organizing at O'Hare Airport and St. Joseph Medical Center." In *Organizing to Win: New Research in Union Strategies,* edited by Kate Bronfenbrenner et al. Ithaca: Cornell University Press. 164–180.

Peterson, Richard B., and Lane Tracy. 1988. "Lessons from Labor-Management Cooperation." *California Management Review* 31 (fall): 41–53.

Pfeffer, Jeffrey, and Gerald E. Salancik. 1978. *The External Control of Organizations: A Resource Dependence Perspective.* New York: Harper and Row.

Precht, Paul. 1997. "Nurses Union Concerned over Use of Assistants." *Boston Business Journal,* June 6–12, 34, 35.

"Public Supports Labor Goals." 1998. *Economic Notes,* Labor Research Association (February): 2.

Purcell, Susan Kaufman. 1993. "What's in NAFTA for US?" *Washington Post,* May 3, A18.

Robinson, Ian. 1994. "NAFTA, Social Unionism, and Labour Movement Power in Canada and the United States." *Relations Industrielles* 49 (4): 657–695.

Rockey, Linda. 1999. "Rx: Organize; More Nurses Look to Unions for Help." *Chicago Tribune,* May 2, C3.

Rogers, Joel. 1993. "Don't Worry, Be Happy: The Post-war Decline of Private Sector Unionism in the United States." In *The Challenge of Restructuring: North American Labor Movements Respond,* edited by Jane Jensen and Rianne Mahon. Philadelphia: Temple University Press. 48–71.

Rohwedder, Cecillie. 1999. "Paying Dues: Once the Big Muscle of German Industry, Unions See It All Sag." *Wall Street Journal,* November 29, A1, A18.

Rose, Joseph B., and Gary N. Chaison. 2000. "North American Unionism in the Twenty-first Century: The Prospects for Revival." Paper presented at the Twelfth World Congress of the International Industrial Relations Association, Tokyo.

Sanger, David E. 1997. "Clinton Embarking on a New Nafta Quest." *New York Times,* September 9, A6.

———. 1998. "Clinton Pressed for Curbs on Steel Imports." *New York Times,* November 6, C2.

———. 1999a. "After Clinton's Push, Questions about Motive." *New York Times,* December 3, A12.

———. 1999b. "Clinton Restricts Imports of Brazilian Steel and Australian Lamb." *New York Times,* July 8, C1, C3.

———. 1999c. "Senate Kills Effort to Impose Tight Limits on Steel Imports." *New York Times,* June 23, A1, C10.

Savage, Lydia. 1996. "Negotiating Common Ground: Labor Unions and Geography in the Service Sector." Ph.D. diss., Clark University.

Schlesinger, Jacob M., and Bernard Wysocki Jr. 1997. "Score Card: UPS Pact Fails to Shift Balance of Power Back toward U.S. Workers." *New York Times,* September 10, A1, A6.

Schoch, James. 1998. "Rising from the Ashes of Defeat and the 1997 'Fast-Track' Fight." Paper presented at the Conference on the Revival of the American Labor Movement, October 17, Cornell University.

Sciacchitano, Katherine. 1997. "Finding the Community in the Union and the Union in the Community: The First-Contract Campaign at Steeltech." In *Organizing to Win: New Research in Union Strategies,* edited by Kate Bronfenbrenner et al. Ithaca: Cornell University Press. 150–163.

Scott, W. Richard. 1987. *Organizations: Rational, Natural, and Open Systems.* Englewood Cliffs, N.J.: Prentice-Hall.

Scott, W. Richard, and John W. Meyer. 1991. "The Organization of Societal Sectors: Propositions and Early Evidence." In *The New Institutionalism in Organizational Analysis,* edited by Walter Powell and Paul J. DiMaggio. Chicago: University of Chicago Press. 108–140.

Sewell, Dan. 1998. "Strike Still Hurting UPS, Workers." Online posting of Associated Press article, labnews@cmsa.berkeley.edu.

Sherer, Peter D., and Huseyin Leblebici. 1990. "Union Membership Rules: What Do They Tell Us about Alternative Union Forms in the Past, Present, and Future?" *Proceedings of the Forty-second Annual Meeting of the Industrial Relations Research Association.* Madison, Wisc.: Industrial Relations Research Association. 74–82.

Shields, Janice. 1995. "'Social Dumping' in Mexico after NAFTA." *Multinational Monitor* 16 (April 1): 20–24.

Shorrock, Tim. 1997. "Nafta Side Agreement Slips into the Fast-Track Spotlight: Today's Meeting Takes on New Significance." *Journal of Commerce,* September 18, 3A.

Shostak, Arthur B. 1991. *Robust Unionism: Innovations and the Labor Movement.* Ithaca: Cornell University Press.

"Sierra Club Opposes Prop. 226." 1998. Online posting, May 20, labnews@cmsa.berkeley.edu.

Smith, Russell E. 1997. "An Early Assessment of the NAFTA Labor Side Accord." In *Proceedings of the Forty-ninth Annual Meeting of the Industrial Relations Research Association*. Madison, Wisc.: Industrial Relations Research Association. 230–236.

Sonnenfeld, Jeffrey A. 1997. "In the Dignity Department, U.P.S. Wins." *New York Times,* August 24, F14.

Stevenson, Richard W. 1997. "Union Misgivings on NAFTA Are Clinton's Latest Worry." *New York Times,* November 5, A8.

Stone, Karen Van Wezel. 1981. "The Post-war Paradigm in American Labor Law." *Yale Law Journal* 90 (June): 1511–80.

———. 1992. "The Legacy of Industrial Pluralism: The Tension between Individual Employment Rights and the New Deal Collective Bargaining System." *University of Chicago Law Review* 59 (spring): 575–674.

Stone, Thomas H., and Daniel G. Gallagher. 1997. "Contingent Workers and Labour Representation: Workers' Disposition and Workers' Prospects." Paper presented at the Third International Conference on Emerging Union Structures: Reshaping Labor Market Institutions, December 3, Australian National University, Canberra.

Strauss, George. 1975. "Union Financial Data." *Industrial Relations* 14 (May): 131–133.

———. 1991. "Union Democracy." In *The State of the Unions,* edited by George Strauss, Daniel G. Gallagher, and Jack Fiorito. Madison, Wisc.: Industrial Relations Research Association. 201–236.

———. 1995. "Is the New Deal Collapsing? With What Might It Be Replaced?" *Industrial Relations* 34 (July): 329–349.

Suchman, Mark C. 1995. "Managing Legitimacy: Strategic and Institutional Approaches." *Academy of Management Review* 20 (July): 571–610.

Sverke, Magnus, and Anders Sjoberg. 1997. "Ideological and Instrumental Union Commitment." In *The Future of Trade Unionism: International Perspectives on Emerging Union Structures,* edited by Magnus Sverke. Aldershot: Ashgate. 277–293.

Tasini, Jonathan. 1986. "Big Labor Tries the Soft Sell." *Business Week,* October 13, 126.

"Teamsters, Labor Win." 1997. Texas AFL-CIO web page January 1, www. texasaflcio.org.

Trade for the Twenty-first Century. 1992. Program for conference sponsored by AFL-CIO, Sierra Club, Public Citizen, Friends of the Earth, and the National Farmers Union, September 8–10, Washington, D.C.

"Trades Cool to Plan Offering New Benefits." 1985. *Engineering News Record,* November 25, 49.

Twedt, Steve. 1996a. "Who's Watching? Hospitals Are Left on Their Own in Setting Standards for Aides." *Pittsburgh Post-Gazette,* February 13, 1.

———. 1996b. "Researcher Is a Hero to Nurses." *Pittsburgh Post-Gazette,* February 14, 1.

Uchitelle, Louis. 1994. "Workers Seek Executive Role, Study Says." *New York Times,* December 5, D1, D10.

———. 1999. "Minimum Wage, City by City." *New York Times,* November 19, C1.

U.S. Department of Labor. 1982. *Report on the Secretary of Labor's Symposium on Cooperative Labor-Management Programs.* Washington, D.C.: U.S. Government Printing Office.

U.S. General Accounting Office. 1993a. *North American Free Trade Agreement: Assessment of Major Issues.* Vol. 1. Washington, D.C.: U.S. General Accounting Office.

———. 1993b. *North American Free Trade Agreement: Assessment of Major Issues.* Vol. 2. Washington, D.C.: U.S. General Accounting Office.

U.S. Secretary of Labor's Task Force on Excellence in State and Local Government through Labor-Management Cooperation. 1996. *Working Together for Public Service.* Washington, D.C.: U. S. Department of Labor.

Verma, Anil, Russell Smith, Marcus Sandver, Kathryn Ready, Morley Gunderson, Lance Compra, and Richard P. Chaykowski. 1996. "Free Trade, Labor Markets, and Industrial Relations: Institutional Developments and the Research Agenda." *Proceedings of the Forty-eighth Annual Meeting of the Industrial Relations Research Association.* Madison, Wisc.: Industrial Relations Research Association. 421–442.

Wayne, Leslie. 1998. "American Steel at the Barricades." *New York Times,* December 10, C1, C8.

———. 1999. "A Divisive Steel-Quota Debate Moves to the Senate." *New York Times,* March 24, C6.

Weinstein, Henry. 1988. "A Textbook Labor Union Campaign." *Los Angeles Times,* May 17, 1.

Weintraub, Sidney. 1997. "In the Debate about NAFTA, Just the Facts Please." *Wall Street Journal,* June 20, A19.

———. 1999. "NAFTA: A Politically Unpopular Success Story." *Los Angeles Times,* February 7, M2.

Wheeler, Jeff. 1997. "Discussion." In *Proceedings of the Forty-ninth Annual Meeting of the Industrial Relations Research Association.* Madison, Wisc.: Industrial Relations Research Association. 243–245.

Wilson Center for Public Research. 1992. "Workers' Views of the Value of Unions." Paper presented at the meeting of the National Union Administrators' Group, May 18, George Meany Center for Labor Studies, Chevy Chase, Md.

Witt, Matt, and Rand Wilson. 1999. "The Teamsters' UPS Strike of 1997: Building a New Labor Movement." *Labor Studies Journal* 24 (spring): 58–72.

Wolff, Joshua. 1997. "UPS Strike: A Victory for Labor." *Indicator* 4 (1): 1–3.

Wolters, Roger S. 1982. "Union-Management Ideological Frames of Reference." *Journal of Management* 8 (fall):21–33.

Wysocki, Bernard, Jr. 1999. "The Outlook: The WTO—The Villain in the Drama It Wrote." *Wall Street Journal,* December 6, A1.

Zullo, Roland, and Stuart Eimer. 2000. "A Profile of a Union-Led Political Coalition." Paper presented at the Fifty-second Annual Meeting of the Industrial Relations Research Association, January 8, Boston.

INDEX

Teamsters, International Brotherhood
of, strike at UPS (*continued*)
   public support for union, 40–42,
      103 n. 2
   settlement, 42
Texas Federation of Teachers-
   Professional Educators Group,
      49, 51
Tracy, L., 4
Trade for the Twenty-first Century, 62
Trade unions. *See* Unions

UAPs. *See* Massachusetts Nurses Association: opposition to unlicensed
   assistive personnel
Uchitelle, L., 20, 27
Union constituencies
   coalition partners, 24–27
   covered nonmembers, 32–33
   employers, 21–24, 53
   general public, 15–17
   members, 28–32
   nonunion workers, 17–20
Union of Electrical, Radio and Machine
   Workers, 26
Union Privilege Benefits
   Corporation, 49
Unions
   cooperation with employers, 4–5
   decline of, 1–2, 90
   institutional environment of, 7–8
   instrumentality, 18–20, 30–32,
      101 nn. 1, 2
   German, 98–99

organizing, 101 n. 2
public opinion of, 4, 15–19
trade policy, 70–72
See also Management of legitimacy;
   Union constituencies
United Food and Commercial
   Workers, 25
United Parcel Service. *See* Teamsters
United States National Labor Relations
   Board, 3, 22
United States-Jordan Trade
   Agreement, 71
United Steelworkers of America, 25
UPS. *See* Teamsters
USA*NAFTA, 60

Verma, A., 67, 107–108 n. 4

Wagner Act. *See* National Labor
   Relations Act
Wayne, L., 102 n. 3
Wells, J., 24
Wheeler, J., 107 n. 4
White, G., 32, 40, 103 n. 6
Wilson Center, 50–51
Wilson, R., 38, 40, 103 n. 1
Wisconsin Citizen Action, 103 n. 5
Witt, M., 38, 40, 103 n. 1
Wolff, J., 39, 41–42, 103 n. 2
Wolters, R., 3
World Trade Organization, 25, 97

Zax, J., 105 n. 9
Zullo, R., 103 n. 5

GARY CHAISON received his Ph.D. from the State University of New York at Buffalo and is professor of industrial relations at the Graduate School of Management, Clark University, Worcester, Massachusetts. His research interests include union structure, government and growth, and comparative industrial relations. He is the author of *Union Mergers in Hard Times: The View from Five Countries* (Cornell University Press) and *When Unions Merge* (Lexington Books).

BARBARA BIGELOW is professor of management at the Graduate School of Management, Clark University. She received her Ph.D. from the Massachusetts Institute of Technology. Her current research interests include organization theory and strategy, and health care administration. She is co-editor of *Health Care Management Review.*